THE TRANSFORMATION OF SEXUALITY

The Transformation of Sexuality
Gender and Identity in Contemporary Youth Culture

THOMAS JOHANSSON
University of Gothenburg, Sweden

ASHGATE

Published by
Ashgate Publishing Limited
Gower House
Croft Road
Aldershot
Hampshire GU11 3HR
England

Ashgate Publishing Company
Suite 420
101 Cherry Street
Burlington, VT 05401-4405
USA

Ashgate website: http://www.ashgate.com

British Library Cataloguing in Publication Data
Johansson, Thomas
  The transformation of sexuality : gender and identity in
  contemporary youth culture
  1. Gender identity - Sweden 2. Youth - Sweden - Attitudes
  3. Youth - Sexual behavior - Sweden
  I. Title
  306.7'6'0835'09485

Library of Congress Cataloging-in-Publication Data
Johansson, Thomas, 1959-
  The transformation of sexuality : gender and identity in contemporary youth culture
/ by Thomas Johansson.
      p. cm.
  Includes bibliographical references and index.
  ISBN: 978-0-7546-4940-3 1. Youth--Sexual behavior. 2. Youth--
Sweden--Sexual behavior. 3. Youth--Social conditions--21st century. 4. Youth--
Attitudes--Cross-cultural studies. 5. Identity (Psychology) 6. Subculture. 7. Sexual
behavior surveys--Sweden. I. Title.

  HQ27.J354 2006
  306.70835'09485--dc22
                                                                    2006025820

ISBN: 978-0-7546-4940-3

Printed and bound in Great Britain by MPG Books Ltd, Bodmin, Cornwall.

Contents

List of Tables

Preface

This book is written within the research project 'Youth, sexuality and gender in transition'. The project was financed by the Swedish research council (FAS). This book is the last one of three volumes (the other two are in Swedish) where the project has been discussed and presented. Two of the chapters are written together with Nils Hammarén, who has also been responsible for all the practical details of the survey. Nils has also read and commented on the whole manuscript. I would like to thank all the people who have been directly or indirectly involved in this project. I also would like to thank all our respondents, who have contributed to this work by giving us information and material.

I am also grateful to Karen Williams, who has translated the main part of this text. Finally I would like to express my gratitude to Philip Lalander, Jesper Andreasson and all the other researchers who contributed to the project.

Thomas Johansson
Gothenburg
15 April 2006

Chapter 1

Introduction

In 1939, sociologist Norbert Elias published his work on the civilization process (Elias 1939/1982). Owing to the war, however, his efforts were forgotten for a time. It was not until 30 years later that the scientific world gave serious consideration to Elias's theory. The basic notion underlying Elias's work is that Western history is also an account of how humankind has gradually developed increasingly sophisticated forms of self-control. In particular this concerns our bodily functions and, thereby, also our sexuality. Elias describes in detail how people are becoming more observant of their own bodily secretions and how they are developing feelings of shame when confronted with them. He considers that people in the Western world are marked by control, discipline and self-consciousness and that these envelop much of everyday life. The process of discipline affects everything from how people regulate their sexuality and bodily secretions to how they speak and behave in their social life. Yet this should not be seen as a development from a spontaneous and natural stage to a civilized stage. Elias considers rather that people have always deferred to some form of discipline, but that these forms have been different throughout human history.

There are many points of contact between Elias and the French philosopher Michel Foucault, whose works include a three-volume work entitled *The History of Sexuality* (Foucault 1978, 1987a, 1987b). Here, Foucault describes how a modern attitude towards sexuality is developing. Modern humans internalize a kind of understanding of what may be viewed as normal as opposed to abnormal sexuality. He considers that, during modern times, sexuality has been made public – through everyday conversations, newspaper articles, scientific articles and sexual guidance information – and that this enables a new form of surveillance and control. In Foucault's thoughts we find elucidation of a paradox: things done for the purpose of liberalization, for example scientific studies of sexuality or sexual guidance information, also entail new methods of control and surveillance. In modern society, people manage their own self-oppression: they are their own controllers. In his book *Civilization and its Discontents* (Freud 1932/1989), Freud describes how this form of discipline is located to the superego, which grows strong because of the growth of a bourgeois hegemony. Put simply, the concept of hegemony refers to a type of monopoly on what is to be considered normal and desirable in a given culture.

In the classical Swedish work *Den kultiverade människan* (*Cultured Man*), ethnologists Jonas Frykman and Orval Löfgren (1979) describe and analyse how the bourgeoisie, during the end of the 19th and beginning of the 20th century, tried to impose their own values on the Swedish peasantry. This was a question of strengthening the bourgeois position of dominance in Swedish society not only by teaching peasants about clock time and schedules, but also by conveying values concerning physicality and sexuality. Frykman and Löfgren sketched a picture of a 'hands-over-the-covers' culture in which the sexual and the physical are seen as objectionable and unclean and in which masturbation is said to lead to serious illness and facial abscesses.

In the bourgeois culture, there was great fear of doing something wrong or of appearing deviant in some way. Considered from a Foucauldian perspective, bourgeois power was everywhere: in the schools, in how dwellings were furnished and designed, in books of etiquette, in the daily press, in the personal advertisements, and so on. If hegemony is to be upheld, people in the culture must be constantly reminded of the natural and rational inherent in what it advocates. Through these constant reminders, a certain normality is segmented in people's consciousness. Breaking with this normality is difficult, not least because it is closely tied to the individual's emotional life – a fear of doing the wrong thing is created. Elias describes this process as follows:

> Fears of this kind play a considerable part in the control to which the child is subject from the beginning, in the prohibitions placed on him. Perhaps only partly conscious in the parents, and partly already automatic, they are transmitted to the child as much by gestures as by words. They continuously add fuel to the fiery circle of inner anxieties, which holds the behaviour and feelings of the growing child permanently within definite limits, binding him to a certain standard of shame and embarrassment, to a specific accent, to particular manners, whether he wishes or not. (Elias 1939/1982: 330)

So, becoming embarrassed and feeling shame derive from a fear of breaking with a certain normality. The line of reasoning pursued thus far, however, does not imply that the individual is totally regulated and controlled by internal directives. A controlled or even uncontrolled acceptance of desire and pleasure is sometimes allowed. Using Elias's term, a kind of escape zone is created to deal with the expectations of normality that each individual lives with. On certain occasions, such as parties, disregard of the norms and values that regulate the sphere of intimacy is accepted. Moreover, imposing taboos tends to create curiosity about the forbidden. In the bourgeois culture that Frykman and Löfgren describe, the consequence of hiding naked flesh was Peeping Tomism.

Elias's and Frykman and Löfgren's analyses of how the body and sexuality are regulated in modern society provide an avenue into the topic of the present book: youth, gender and sexuality. While we see today a picture in which young people's sexual thoughts and actions are characterized by experimentation and freedom, free and equal sexuality between men and women is still restricted and obstructed in many ways. For instance, research shows that young women are subjected, to a great extent, to sexism, oppression and dominance (Jeffner 1997; Holland et al 1998).

In approaching the present topic, we notice that it is intersected by prejudices, ideological notions and desire. Young people are both actors and objects. They shape their own sexuality and form their own desire, but they are also subjected to sexualization and exploitation. On advertisement billboards we see perfect, well-trained young bodies. Most of these bodies belong to young women, but it is becoming more common to aestheticize men, too, thereby transforming them into objects (Nixon 1996, Johansson 1998).

The present book constitutes an attempt to get behind media images and prejudices. Based on an extensive survey, but primarily on in-depth studies of different groups of young people, we will explore some central questions concerning young people's sexuality. Considering the work of authors such as Norbert Elias and Michel Foucault, it may be worth reflecting on the question of just how regulated young people's sexuality actually is; and what, exactly, is meant by sexual freedom.

The book begins with a section that presents several central theories of sexuality and society. This chapter brings to the fore some of the perspectives and questions used throughout the book. The central question concerns the extent to which we may speak today about sexual liberation, or whether we instead should view human sexuality as increasingly controlled and manipulated by commercial forces. This chapter places this book within a field of sexuality and gender studies. Thereafter the books is divided into several different parts.

The second part of the book – 'Youth, Gender and Sexuality: Positions and Transitions' – consists of two chapters, each treating different aspects of young people's construction of gender, sexuality and identity. The first chapter deals with Scandinavian and Anglo-Saxon school and youth research. Much of the discussion on young people's sexuality has centred on what is happening in and around schools. Thus, educational research on young people has often started specifically with the classroom and what happens there, only later to expand its interest to the youth culture in general. In this chapter, we discuss the different depictions of young people's sexuality that emerge from this research. Chapter 4 brings forward changes within youth culture research, starting in the 1970s and then gradually presenting a more up-to-date picture of research on these issues.

The third part of the book – 'Desire and Identity in Contemporary Sweden' – contains the main part of this book. Here the Swedish study is presented in several chapters, each dealing with specific issues. Chapter 5 is largely based on data from an extensive Swedish quantitative study of young people's outlooks on and relations to their own sexuality. The major areas dealt with here are: fidelity/infidelity, love, homosexuality, pornography and beauty ideals. We discuss the data in the light of other relevant research findings. In Scandinavia and the Anglo-Saxon world, there are a number of studies similar to ours; we consider these in relation to our study. The following chapter focuses more specifically on how young people look upon and consume pornography.

In Chapter 7, we deal primarily with young women's struggle for independence and gender equality. We use examples from a great variety of empirical studies, and discuss the relation between politics, sexuality and gender. Emerging from this chapter is a tremendously active, self-confident and potent young woman. This image is intended to function as a contrast to the young female images often appearing in research, the media and other public spheres.

The following chapter deals with the construction of masculinity. It takes up a number of current tendencies and changes among young men. In this chapter, we use empirical examples from case studies of young feminist men, women playing on women's soccer teams and bisexual men. The central question is: what changes are we able to discern among young men today?

Chapter 9 deals with questions concerning different norm systems and cultural perceptions of sexuality. On the basis of several case studies of young immigrant men and women, we will discuss issues of power, ethnicity and sexuality. This chapter also makes connections between sexuality, gender and space.

In the next part of the book, I will sum up all these different discussions, and once again return to the issues and questions raised at the beginning of the book. The purpose here is both to draw some general conclusions and to indicate the need for further research in certain areas. In this section I have also added a chapter that looks more carefully into issues around the media and sexuality. The last part of the book contains a more thorough discussion of methodological issues.

The present book is largely based on empirical data from an extensive Swedish research project on youth, gender and sexuality. The project has taken a fairly broad approach and has tried, using surveys and a number of qualitative in-depth studies to capture developments among today's Swedish teenagers (16–19 years of age). This broad approach has also been combined with a number of group interviews with young people as well as a number of more specific qualitative in-depth studies. The survey was distributed among young people attending schools in two Swedish cities: Gothenburg and Kalmar. A total of over 1,300 surveys were completed and returned (see Chapters 5 and 6).

The purpose of the various in-depth studies has been to obtain a broad as well as an extensive picture of how young people belonging to different groups and constellations view and relate to their own sexuality. Among other groups, we have spoken with political lesbians, male handball players, female soccer players, young Christians, immigrant young people and young men who view themselves as feminists (Johansson and Lalander 2003, Johansson 2005).

The interested reader will find in the Appendix a more thorough presentation and discussion of the empirical basis of the study. I would finally like to stress that in writing the book my sole ambition has not been to present our own investigation, but instead to use it as a point of departure in discussing current Scandinavian and Anglo-Saxon research on youth, sexuality and gender.

PART I
Scientia Sexualis

Chapter 2

Pleasure and Desire in Modern Times

It is in this sense that the sexological account of sexual identity can be seen as an imposition, a crude tactic of power designed to obscure a real sexual diversity with the myth of sexual destiny. (Weeks 1987: 37)

In one sense, it may point to the fact that overall inequalities in the relationship between man and woman handed down to us by our culture are playing havoc with many people's lives, both men's and women's. (Hite 1981: xvii)

The first quotation is taken from an article by feminist historian Jeffrey Weeks. Here, he sharply criticizes sexology. Weeks asks whether sexology – the purpose of which is to increase our knowledge of human sexuality – doesn't actually result in increased sexual repression and the categorization and compartmentalization of individuals rather than in their liberation. This is a perfectly apt question based on a critical theory of gender and sexuality. The second quotation is from sexologist Shere Hite's well-known study of male sexuality. She states that the sex-role stereotypes that still dominate our ideas about gender and sexuality tend to diminish people and to reduce their ability to grow and mature sexually. On a superficial level, both Weeks and Hite seem to have the same ambitions for their work on sexuality: to work toward liberation and to counteract sexual repression. Yet these two scholars actually belong to two completely separate schools of thought and research that have developed around issues of human sexuality.

While Weeks explores the historical and cultural factors that help to form our sexuality, Hite focuses on detailed studies of sexual behaviour and expression: how often do you have sex? Do men like oral sex? Is masturbation a frequently occurring behaviour? How is an orgasm experienced? And so on. Weeks's work concerns putting sexuality into a cultural and social context, while Hite's research deals with detailed investigations of factual and concrete forms of sexual expression. Thus, the scientific study of human sexuality has different manifestations and focuses on different aspects of the phenomenon. Weeks criticizes the scientification that sexology has been responsible for, yet he is also partly a victim of the same process. His work too may be used to legitimize a particular view of sexuality.

In late-modern society, science is no longer a project that takes place inside an ivory tower – it is not a glass bead game, but instead a reflexive process involving scientists, the people they study and journalists. The study of sexuality has also helped to create sexualities, that is, to shape and develop our view of sexuality and our behaviour as sexual beings. This is also one of the strong points made by Michel Foucault. Here, we may speak of a widespread scientification of sexuality.

According to Foucault, science – not least sexology – has helped to create new combinations of power, physicality and sexuality. Scientific classifications are transformed into 'truths'. In certain cases, this has led to strong opposition to an excessively narrow way of looking at sexuality, in other cases, to people's use of scientific categories and tools in the active formation of their own sexuality. Thus, modern forms of sexuality are largely products of science, which implies the disappearance of our ability to speak of any form of pure or authentic sexuality.

The media constitute another important actor with a great influence on how sexuality is presented and staged. In the media, we find large numbers of talk shows, documentaries and films containing vivid portrayals and pictures of human sexuality. People are deluged with these imaginary products, and though it is difficult to determine the degree to which and in what way people are affected, we can certainly establish that this media world helps to shape our image of sexuality, physicality and gender. The sexual education supplied by the media – thus, 'mediaized' sexuality – has in many respects replaced science as well as replacing the sex education taught in the schools.

Today, viewing sexuality as something natural – something that just exists and works – is not completely self-evident. It is instead the case that sexologists, gender scholars, feminists, journalists, psychologists and sociologists help to create and construct, both consciously and unconsciously, our picture of sexuality. When you study sexuality, you become a part of this apparatus. The entire contemporary discussion on sexuality – perhaps that on young people's sexuality in particular – is intersected by different discourses and theories concerning how we can or even should view sexuality and physicality.

The question is to what degree it is at all possible to differentiate between the sexual moments of everyday life and the discourses and images that shape human sexuality in today's society. Both of these realities have become increasingly blurred and have come to form a complex cultural fabric. In this chapter, we will follow the path from Foucault's studies of sexuality to Baudrillard's theories of postmodern sexuality. This will form the foundation of a discussion and analysis of sexual narrations and expressions in our time, with particular focus on young people's sexuality.

Scientia Sexualis

In his three-volume work *The History of Sexuality* (1981, 1987a, 1987b), Foucault starts from the frequently occurring hypothesis that there was an increase in sexual repression during the bourgeois epoch. He does not consider that this hypothesis is incorrect, but that it needs appreciable modification. Foucault wishes to get behind this hypothesis of repression and analyse the connections between power, sexuality and gender that create everyday pleasures and that give desire its cultural forms. Talk about gender and about sexuality has gradually become more qualified, nuanced and interwoven with power. In modern societies, interest in the sexual has gradually increased.

Talk about sex and, later on, the entrance of science – with its tendency towards classification and its frenetic search for more and different sexual types, sexual deviations and peculiarities – led to the scientification of everyday sexuality. A sexual landscape was created, filled with all manner of creations: Binet's fetishists, Krafft-Ebing's zoophiles and zooerasts, Rohleder's auto-monosexualists, mixoscopophiles, gynecomasts, presbyophiles, sexoesthetic inverts and dyspareunist women (Foucault 1978).

> These fine names for heresies referred to a nature that was overlooked by the law, but not so neglectful of itself that it did not go on producing more species, even where there was no order to fit them into. The machinery of power that focused on this whole alien strain did not aim to suppress it, but rather to give it an analytical visible, and permanent reality: it was implanted in bodies, slipped in beneath modes of conduct, made into a principle of classification and intelligibility, established as a *raison d'être* and a natural order of disorder. Not the exclusion of these thousands aberrant sexualities, but the specification, the regional solidification of each one of them. The strategy behind this dissemination was to strew reality with them and incorporate them into the individual. (Foucalt 1978: 44)

In this scientification of sexuality lay a great duplicity. The order that had been established was ostensible and, therefore, able to serve as a point of departure for the active formation of new sexual identities, which in their turn could be used as a platform for offering resistance to the excessively narrow view of sexuality found in psychiatry and sexology. Thus, the original scientific ambition led to the creation of new pleasures and new, intricate interplays between body, sexuality and gender.

There emerged rather directly a relationship between the old type of confessions and science. Talk about sexuality increased dramatically; it multiplied and was soon found everywhere. In modern society, we want to know; we want detailed information about sexuality. We want all this in order to develop our knowledge of sex and human sexuality. Fascination with the physical and endeavours to reveal secrets certainly took on scientific forms, but when we study pictures from the early days of psychiatry, we see how men cast their greedy eyes over the hysterical female bodies that were used as illustrative material. Thus, the will to know is not an irreproachable drive, but must be interpreted within the framework of a particular society and the rules of pleasure that constitute the normative means of control in that societal system.

According to Foucault, however, speaking about pleasure outside or beyond power is a hopeless project. Pleasure, desire, power and coercion are woven together to form something we then call sexuality. Thus, it is difficult to separate one aspect from the other. Is rape only a matter of male aggression and not a matter of sexuality? On the basis of Foucault's ideas, we might say that it is probably a question of a sexuality in which power and pleasure have taken on socially unacceptable forms. In Foucault's view, it is impossible to talk about pure sexuality. Even when discussing resistance, we are always relating to and interwoven into a power network.

Resistance often constitutes the other side of power relations.

Where there is power, there is resistance, and yet, or rather consequently, this resistance is never in a position of exteriority in relation to power [...] These points of resistance are present everywhere in the power network. Hence there is no single locus of great Refusal, no soul of revolt, source of all rebellions, or pure law of the revolutionary. Instead there is a plurality of resistances, each of them a special case: resistances that are spontaneous, savage, solitary, concerted, rampant, or violent. Still others that are quick to compromise, interested, or sacrificial; by definition, they can only exist in the strategic field of power relations. (Foucault 1978: 95)

The interplay between power, resistance and pleasure is extremely complicated. We may never speak of obvious power relations in which super- and subordination are clearly established, but instead of degrees of power and of a dynamic interaction between power and resistance. In many respects, Foucault's way of approaching these issues leaves us in a moral vacuum. We find ourselves in a place beyond good and evil, while it is also possible to draw certain radically moral conclusions based on the line of reasoning he pursues.

Has scientists' eagerness to press people for confessions resulted in increased repression? Foucault's point is that it is certainly arguable that the apparatus of repression has become increasingly effective and consistent, but that we must also consider that this apparatus has simultaneously created new pleasures and that where there is power, there is often resistance. This is a question, therefore, of a flexible and changeable system of power relations, in which extensive, but never total, dominance relations emerge.

Foucault identifies and shows considerable interest in four different characters: the hysterical women, the masturbating child, the Malthusian couple and the perverted man. These four types constitute anchor points for much of the research and knowledge about sexuality developed during the 19th century. This is also where psychoanalysis enters the scene as a kind of liberator of sexuality. Freud and psychoanalysis worked to do away with the repression that was thought to help create the hysterical woman. Toward the end of the first volume of *The History of Sexuality* (1978), Foucault implies a kind of criticism of psychoanalysis, or, more correctly, he tries to show how even this scientific discipline may be placed within a narrative on different historical patterns of repression and sexuality.

In the second and third volumes of *The History of Sexuality*, Foucault looks back at antiquity (Foucault 1987a, 1987b). He explores the sexual patterns that emerged, particularly among free men. He shows how sexuality was arranged in an active life pattern, as a way of approaching the self that included physical training, diet and sexual pleasure – a way of caring for the body that, to be sure, took place within certain moral and ethical frameworks, but that also allowed great freedom with respect to how people viewed such things as infidelity and sexual excesses. Unfortunately, Foucault was not able to complete his work on the history of sexuality before his death. It stops just before he begins to look at the influence of Christianity on patterns of sexuality. It is possible to read these last two volumes as arguments in favour of the notion that the sexuality of antiquity was relatively open, though Foucault also shows clearly that patterns of dominance are found even here.

Foucault managed to suggest a great deal about the path he intended to take through the history of sexuality, but he also left many loose ends. What was his view on the role of psychoanalysis or on the sexual liberation of the 1960s and 1970s? How would Foucault have interpreted the rest of the story up to the present era and its mediaized sexuality?

Hyperreal Sexuality

Seduction lies in the transformation of things into pure appearance. (Baudrillard 1977/1990: 117)

When everything is sexual, nothing is sexual any more and sex loses its determinants. (Baudrillard 1993a: 9)

The historical process Foucault analyses in the first volume of *The History of Sexuality* (1978) focuses on the scientification of sexuality that is taking place in modern society. Today, the scientific apparatus – particularly the disciplines of medicine, sexology and psychology – is mapping and exploring all the nooks and crannies of sexuality. If we move on to a contemporary theorist and philosopher such as Jean Baudrillard, we find ourselves in the media age, a period that Foucault was not able to write about or analyse. Talk about sexuality is now transformed into the flow of pictures and phantasms produced and distributed via various media (Baudrillard 1977/1990, 1993a, 1993b).

As a result of the confession, we have now developed our knowledge of most aspects of human sexuality. Sexuality has been explored, penetrated and colonized. It is hard to imagine being able to shock people today – getting them to react strongly to how sexuality is portrayed and stressed in the public sphere. Still, moral reactions and even moral panic do occur, but die out rather quickly and disappear in the media roar. The fact that people cannot be shocked, however, does not imply a lack of prejudices, moral stands or of repressive outlooks on sexuality in our society. These phenomena are simply manifested in ways other than the classic Victorian variation on sexual morality.

When sexuality is subjected to total penetration and becomes an ingredient in everything from soap operas to talk shows, what is there left to keep secret or protect? When seduction becomes an increasingly abstract process – a kind of hallucinatory pleasure of the signs, a fascination with the superficial or with intrusive cameras' pictures of genitals in action – what is there left to be seduced by? Baudrillard takes us to the end of the journey. According to him, when we have done all this, we have also eradicated what we used to call sexuality. The sexual is emptied of all meaning, but we are still left with our fascination, our expectation that there are more limits to be exceeded and that the search must continue.

Sexuality has never been more realistic, represented as accurately as possible, so that every detail is included in obtrusive portrayals of people's sexual existence. Current media technology provides undreamt-of possibilities to conduct exhaustive studies of human beings' physical relations. Certainly, this total demystification of human sexuality also defuses it, but the fall-out of this are new mythologies, new fantasies and new attempts to make the sexual secret. These novelties, however, only constitute temporary barriers to the hyperreal exploration of sexuality; they are soon drawn into the media roar.

In today's society, talking about a true sexuality or something authentic is problematic. The scientific revolution and successful exploration of sexuality during the 19th and 20th centuries constituted one of the starting points of the continued study of the sexual during the latter half of the 20th century. Today, scientific observation is supplemented with the media's capacity to penetrate even more deeply all aspects of sexuality. In talk shows, various aspects of the sexual are literally talked to pieces. This is not just confined to talking, but pictures are also used to study in detail different kinds of facial expressions, body movements and emotional expressions. Yet, while boundaries, distinctions and moral norms are disintegrating in the media world, we can sometimes see in everyday life that a repressive, normative sexuality has gained or is gaining a greater foothold. How can we reconcile these two aspects?

Baudrillard would probably not have concerned himself with discussing the relation between a simulated reality, for example, the media world, and our social reality. What he stresses is how the form itself – the medium is the message – shapes our perception and our consciousness. Today, we must also examine both the media world's images and everyday life's lived reality. Though we are able to observe increased experimentation with sexuality in the media, signs of the opposite also exist – the cultivation of a number of very traditional conceptions of gender and sexuality. Thus, in this way, we may say that everyday life is both conservative and radically pioneering.

It is difficult to say exactly how we should apply Baudrillard's ideas to concrete empirical data. As a thought experiment, we can imagine how young people's sexuality and views on, for example, anal sex are shaped by the pornographic industry and the porn films they see. For instance, it has been shown that young men who have watched porn films are more likely to practice anal sex than are those who have not watched such films (Häggström-Nordin 2005). The images that colonize our inner world tend to influence us, in exactly what ways we do not always know, but it is conceivable that our sex lives sometimes collapse into the world of pornography. We can follow Baudrillard's reasoning this far, but even if we find more and more support for his ideas, it is still impossible to imagine a total dissolution of the distinction between everyday life and the media.

If, as Baudrillard claims, the USA and Disneyland are the same thing, then perhaps the world of pornography corresponds in the same way to people's actual sexuality. If the boundaries between the imaginary and the social no longer apply, then the boundaries between eroticism and porno, between good and evil as well as good and bad sexuality will also collapse. If we conduct a thought experiment in the spirit of Baudrillard, we can imagine that the porn industry is actually the reality in which we live – the world that provides the pictures, sexual narratives and subject matter for people's sexuality. We will return to these questions later, after a digression on how contemporary human beings create their sexuality.

Sex as Narrative and Manual

In *The Transformation of Intimacy*, Giddens (1992) discusses the changes that people's intimate relationships have undergone during modernity. Contemporary love relations are increasingly characterized by openness. Relations and sexuality are not given in advance, but are instead open to negotiations, shifts and sometimes even dramatic transformations. These transformations place greater demands on people to keep up-to-date and to read the latest manuals with advice on how they should cultivate their love and sex lives (Hawkes 1996).

These new manuals need not always be books, but may equally be the content of soap operas or magazines. The duplicity that characterizes all attempts to define, categorize, study, present and give shape to sexuality is something that contemporary humankind must live with. Yet when is this a matter of repression and when is it a matter of freedom, desire and acknowledgement of sexuality? The duplicity that Foucault once pointed out would appear to be something we must learn to live with (Weeks 1985).

We may ask ourselves whether everyday life and people in general have developed in the direction of what Giddens calls pure relations. Or, we may ask whether sexual experimentation, adventure, full expression or the worry-free life – that is, everything that would seem to characterize postmodern humankind – has also marked the sexuality of contemporary humankind to increasingly greater degrees. Isn't it still the case that sexuality is surrounded by sexual taboos, boundaries, morals and other directives? When Bauman describes his postmodern sexuality, it is precisely this sexuality free from responsibility that he stresses.

> Eroticism cut free from its reproductive and amorous constraints fits the bill very well; it is as if it were made to measure for the multiple, flexible, evanescent identities of postmodern men and women. Sex free of reproductive consequences and stubborn, lingering love attachments can be securely enclosed in the frame of an episode, as it will engrave no deep grooves on the constantly re-groomed face being thus insured against limiting the freedom of further experimentation. (Bauman 1999: 27)

We can compare this picture to that presented by Ken Plummer (1996) in a number of texts on the reflexive and ethical individual. Choosing and recognizing one's own freedom – in some sense – is not necessarily the same as developing an inconsiderate attitude. The difficulty inherent in determining the promiscuous, the affirming and the sexual is something that permeates many of the texts and research dealing with human sexuality.

What Foucault, Baudrillard and Bauman touch upon is a theme connected to the idea of a *post-emotional society* – a society in which emotional life has become increasingly undermined, affected, outstripped and mediaized (Mestrović 1997).

We no longer see the fascination with confession that Foucault discusses, but have instead developed what Simmel (1900/1990) calls a blasé attitude. Yet people still continue to confess and tell their sexual stories. Interpreting these stories has become increasingly difficult. According to Plummer, people find their inspiration and models for their storytelling in the media and in the culture. There are, therefore, no true narratives, only narratives. Could it be the case that this telling has become somewhat mechanical – that narratives come nowhere near any form of authenticity?

If sex has become more and more calculated – something used instrumentally or perhaps something interconnected with the imaginary and with the media images we are fed on a daily basis – then a shift from everyday life to the simulated world has taken place. If everything that reminds us of 'the natural' – for example bodily secretions and odours – is experienced as strange, as something that must be eliminated, where does that leave us? Perhaps, in the end, people will stop having physical sex and start engaging in telephone sex or having their relationships on the Internet instead of in a problem-filled reality (Kroker and Kroker 1988).

Sexuality is, and has perhaps always been, problematic. Waves of sexual liberation are followed by the growth of new restrictions and new forms of repressive sexual morals (Dew 1996; McLaren 1999). Here we can observe a constant interplay. For instance, what seems to be an assertion of a feminist outlook on gender and sexuality, which should stand for liberation and a struggle against repression, may easily turn into a reinforcement of the phenomenon being combated and may result in a new type of moralism (Dew 1996).

The fact that people are currently being deluged with sexual pictures and narratives – that 'the clinical gaze' has become an everyday starting point for formulating views and politics concerning sexuality – and that this does not keep them from acknowledging their sexuality and enjoying sex and their bodies, renders analysis of these phenomena considerably more complicated. Here, we are entering a field that has been travelled length and breadth by early pioneers and explorers who have mapped, studied and said both intelligent and extremely simplistic things about human sexuality. In the midst of this crossfire, we are trying to discover something, to say something about this field of intimacy, closeness and physicality. But what is there left to be said? Has everything important already been expressed?

Perhaps it is the case that the stories people tell remain within the framework of the socially desirable – the acceptable – and thus actually hide the 'truth', giving a skewed picture of human sexuality. Does there still exist, then, a normative sexuality, a kind of hegemonic ditto? Or can we instead observe an enormous differentiation – a landscape of sexual freedom? In Freud's time, this was a question of neuroses and of the repression aimed at sexuality. The perverse, polymorphic individual emerged as the other side of neurosis and repression. This was a person who acknowledged all aspects of his/her sexuality and body, an individual who had not subordinated these things to the genitals or to the paradigm of reproduction.

The Epoch of Perversions

During Freud's time, the late 19th and early 20th century, perversions were thought to be a response to the sexual repression that was widespread, particularly in bourgeois circles. It was the time of the hysterical woman and the compulsive man. By reading perversions as responses to a repression that affected people in different ways – as signs of how sexuality still reared its 'ugly' head – psychoanalysis helped to place perversions in the stream of sexuality.

What was then called a perversion is now often viewed as an identity. Moreover, today the word perversion has an unpleasant ring, which is perhaps not so remarkable if we look at its history. Consider, for example, homosexuality. Freud certainly never condemned homosexuality. Furthermore, he started from a theory based on the notion of early bisexuality. Yet despite this, he felt that homosexuality was a perversion – an error in the path toward formation of a mature genital sexuality. Correctly used and read through historical glasses, Freud's ideas and psychoanalysis constitute a path from biological determinism to psychological constructivism, though psychoanalysis never takes the full step towards recognizing those behaviours that are called perversions.

The question of what is actually pathological and what is identity politics has become increasingly difficult to get straight, investigate and answer. Behaviours previously considered perversions are now identities. The question is also whether the mature sexual person is a character who belongs to the past. Open relationships, sexual experimentation, boundary-crossing behaviour and 'perversions' are things people can indulge in and enjoy, with certain reservations. But psychiatry, psychology and the control apparatus are on top of these matters, constantly formulating new diagnoses and developing and refining their classifications of human behaviour.

When psychiatrists and psychologists begin talking about narcissism and narcissistic disorders as new illnesses, we soon acquire a new set of symptoms in connection with sexuality. It seems as though new opportunities for moralizing and for elaborating diagnoses of deviant sexuality are always emerging. The diffuse diagnosis of narcissism often includes a section on acting out and irresponsible sexuality (Ronningstam 1988). The narcissistic individual never develops genuine intimate relationships, but instead uses other people to meet his/her own needs. He/she is exhibitionistic, flirts wildly and acts out his/her sexuality without any moral reservations.

At the same time, however, we may wonder whether narcissism, as it is often described, isn't actually a common condition for contemporary humankind. The vulnerability, ambivalence, transparency and searching that mark this personality type are traits and expressions that would seem to characterize many individuals. When sexuality is acted out in relatively free forms, it poses an immediate threat to social cohesion, family ties and society. Thus, it must be subject to some kind of control. Yet the boundaries are wider today. People can acknowledge their sexuality, come out as homosexuals and test their sexual limits, but there is often a price.

How far can one go? This varies a great deal across different social and cultural environments (Ziehe 1989).

In contemporary society, it is more permissible to acknowledge and express one's sexuality in narratives and in other forms. At the same time, however, we may ask whether this acknowledgement has not pushed sexuality into a corner. If all the secrets have been revealed and if it is no longer possible to hide anything, what is to become of curiosity, excitement and defiance? If sexuality has become transparent, mediaized, exposed and legitimate, where then is the mystery?

This brief theoretical section is intended as an opening to the research that will be presented and analysed here. Starting from and inspired by the ideas of thinkers such as Foucault and Baudrillard, we will study how young people think, act and relate to sexuality and the construction of gender. Based on Foucault's ideas about power and discipline, we will study, define, delimit and set up frameworks for sexuality and gender. Although we live today in a time when it is permissible, in many countries, to acknowledge one's sexuality and desire, this does not imply that any type of behaviour may be staged without problems. There are always limits.

Considering Baudrillard's ideas, it is interesting to study how media representations and the imaginary world infiltrate and permeate the construction of gender and sexuality. What type of narrative is possible and doable today? What models do young people use when telling their stories and sharing their experiences and feelings?

This book is explorative in nature. It is about seeing and deconstructing part of the more predominant societal narratives on youth, gender and sexuality. It is also about providing a picture of today's scientific discussions on these issues.

PART II
Youth, Gender and Sexuality:
Positions and Transitions

Chapter 3

Gender, Sexuality and Institutional Settings

In Sweden the beginning of 2005 was marked by intense discussions about whether a newly formed feminist party would have any chance of success in the 2006 general election.[1] Another burning question has concerned parental leave insurance and the possibility of getting fathers to stay at home with infants and small children. We see today the growth of a new and greater awareness of the meaning of gender in various social contexts. Discussions are constantly pursued concerning men's and women's different economic, social and cultural conditions. There are also great ambitions to create a fairer and more equal society. These ambitions are manifested in various ways, from political efforts to young women's struggle against the pornography industry.

It is almost impossible to avoid taking a stand on issues of gender, power and justice. This does not imply, however, that we are currently approaching a just and equal society. If we look more closely at statistics on family, the labour market and education, we soon see that many classic gender patterns tend to be persistent (Lundgren 2001). Thus, we are living in a time of paradox. There is a great deal of talk about equality, and certainly things are happening, but at the same time it is easy to identify many *inequalities*.

How do young people deal with these paradoxes? What is the situation in schools? Has the societal struggle for equality made any clear impressions on the attitudes of teachers and schools? What is the relation between young people's worlds and the world of the schools? Are they marked by different social realities or by the same type of patterns? And, above all, in what way are gender and sexuality staged and reproduced in these contexts?

We will focus in particular on how attitudes towards and conceptions and understandings of sexuality affect and form young people's everyday lives. We take our point of departure as the world of school, but gradually broaden this perspective, especially in the next chapter.

There has been a longstanding interest in studying differences between the sexes. Up until the 1970s, educational scientists and pedagogues were engaged in studying and establishing *sex differences*. Measures have been made and it has been shown that young men and women are different in many respects. These differences include: academic achievement, choice of subject, interests and motivation. This

---

1   The feminist party was not very successful in the 2006 general election. So, in the end this was more of a media event than a real political success story.

research has helped to establish the existence of differences, but has shown little interest in developing alternative interpretations and explanatory models or, for that matter, critical perspectives.

During the 1970s, gender-conscious scholars began to take a serious interest in the world of school. Research on sex differences was seen in relation to a broader discussion on power and gender. During the 1970s and 1980s, this research was largely focused on analysing how women's subordination is reproduced in the schools in various ways. It was shown in a number of classroom studies that boys received more attention and support than girls did. This research confirmed the picture of a school system in which boys and girls were viewed and treated differently (Einarsson and Hultman 1984; Öhrn 2000).

In a major Swedish investigation from the beginning of the 1980s (Einarsson and Hultman 1984: 15; the title translates as *Good Morning, Boys and Girls: On Language and Gender in Schools*) we find the following example of how five-year-old Tanja and seven-year-old Lars talk about gender and occupations:

Lars: You know what I'm gonna be when I grow up?
Tanja: No.
Lars: A fireman.
Tanja: I'm gonna be an ambulance driver.
Lars: Okay. (Pause)
Tanja: But I can't.
Lars: Why not?
Tanja: 'Cause I'm a girl.
Lars: Yeah, but Ingrid's a doctor.
Tanja: Yeah, maybe I can be a lady doctor.
Lars: No, maybe Ingrid isn't really a doctor.

The report later shows how boys and girls of different ages take on their respective roles. These patterns are developed early and later confirmed again and again throughout the school years.

The picture changed somewhat during the 1990s, however. Scholars began to talk about changes – about how girls' performance in many school subjects was now better than boys'. In several European countries this discovery led to strong reactions (Öhrn 2000; Francis and Skelton 2001). The talk then turned to the vulnerability of boys, to the lack of male models in the schools and to how this situation had to be improved. The reactions in Sweden were not as great as in the UK, for example, but similar discussions were pursued (Öhrn 1991, 2000). The question is to what extent we may really speak of any drastic changes in the balance of power between the sexes. We will return to this discussion later on.

Although we can see today increased awareness of how gender differences are reproduced and created in the schools, this does not imply the existence of a standard policy concerning these issues. In her article, Swedish pedagogue Elisabet Öhrn (2000) discusses a report from the Ministry of Education, published as late as 1993. The report affirms the importance of teachers and other school staff learning about the gender differences that do exist so that they may base their efforts on this knowledge. A biological perspective on gender predominates in the report.

What is the magnitude of these changes? What we see in Scandinavian as well as Anglo-Saxon research is that the results of different studies are conflicting. Some scholars claim, based on their studies, that polarized gender patterns remain, nearly unaltered, while others are able to show actual changes.[2] For instance, there is strong support for the claim that girls now have a more prominent and active role in the classroom and in the school. Another topic concerns how many young men perform poorly in school, thereby ending up in a marginalized and vulnerable position. Research more focused on young people's sexuality tends to give a very polarized and, in our view, stereotyped picture of how young men and women relate to their own bodies, desire and sex. We will study and discuss these findings later on.

In this chapter we will look more closely at research on how gender and sexuality are reproduced in and outside the classroom. However, in the next chapter we turn towards more general research on youth, sexuality, gender and identity. The studies presented concern in one way or another how teenagers themselves relate to and view the significance of gender and sexuality.

Today, the hidden curriculum is no longer particularly hidden. There is great awareness of how different power patterns affect and set the agenda for schoolwork. But this awareness is only *partial*, that is, we have only partly seen through the existing gender and power patterns. Teachers still attach different traits and abilities to the sexes. While some teachers are actively working to counteract the worst effects of inequality, others are less committed. Moreover, it is the young people themselves who, to a great extent, help to strengthen these diametrical gender patterns. For instance, our research shows that young men have a great tendency to reproduce patterns of homophobia and sexism (Hammarén and Johansson 2001, 2002). This does not imply, however, that all young men participate in such reproduction. There is, of course, considerable variation in their attitudes and behaviours.

Questions of sexuality, the body, gender and identity are intimately and complexly interwoven during the teenage years. Many of the demarcations and hierarchies that are established are based on how young people approach their sexual identity. We see today how several previously rather rigid understandings of sexuality and gender have been called into question. This creates new possibilities and probably new problems as well.

Gender cultures

In much of the existing literature on youth, gender and the schools, we find descriptions of two different *gender cultures*. This pattern is evident in a great portion of the school and youth research from the 1970s and 80s, but these descriptions of gender differences are also found in various forms in the current research literature.

---

2   See for example Holland et al (1998), Öhrn (2000), Frosh et al (2002), Johansson (2005).

Naturally, there is considerable support for this picture, and this support is mainly of three types:

- *Empirical support*. There are a large number of empirical studies showing that boys and girls behave differently, perform differently, have different interests and think in different ways.
- *Everyday life*. Great numbers of everyday observations – at daycare, home, the workplace and school – support the picture of distinct and clear gender differences.
- *Developmental psychology*. Many developmental psychologists claim that boys and girls develop in different ways and that it is important to consolidate a firm and clear gender identity.
- *Feminist theory*. Much of the existing statistics show clear and reliable gender differences. This holds true regardless of which area we consider. From a feminist or gender studies perspective, these differences are interpreted in terms of power and patriarchal patterns.

Recently, however, scholars have been trying to help nuance this picture. A number of studies have even shown changes in the balance of power between the sexes. Although these changes should not be taken as support for the notion that we now live in a society characterized by equality, such tendencies must be taken into account. The upshot of this is that we, for example, must give shape to new theoretical tools or at least modify our old ones.

As gender scholars, we must develop the ability to study and discuss conflicting results. The picture is complicated. What is important is having a double gaze – being able to see both continuity and change. We will first give a brief and rough picture of how young men and women have been described in the research. Thereafter, we will try to contribute to the discussion on these partly true, but also stereotyped portrayals of gender.

These images of gender were quite common in research performed in the 1970s and 80s, but it is also possible to discover these kinds of stereotypes in contemporary research on gender and youth.

Young men organize themselves into *gangs*. These gangs are often hierarchically ordered and have clear leaders. In order to become a member of a gang, you must complete an initiation rite, which is often quite dramatic in nature. The new member is subjected to some type of test, which may well consist of merciless and humiliating treatment. The young man must learn to take his place in the strictly ordered hierarchy. He shall be socialized into *masculinity*, and such socialization is sometimes manifested in the cultivation of homophobia, sexism and violence. The picture of young male sexuality emerging here tends to take on a stereotypical and one-dimensional character. What are often lacking are more complex and multifaceted pictures of how young men view the body, sexuality and gender.

Young women organize themselves into so-called *friend dyads*. These exclusive friendship relations form the point of departure for contacts with other same-sex friends and with young men. While young men often get together on the streets, young women tend to see each other in the private sphere. They cultivate their romantic dreams and develop an intimate form of communication in the girls' room. This type of sociality may indeed underlie collective forms of social relations and solidarity with other young women, but the authoritative organizational principles we often see in young men are conspicuous by their absence. With regard to sexuality, the pictures presented here are characterized by their lack of sexuality, desire and physicality.

A great deal of current feminist research stresses border crossing and the fact that gender is a social and cultural construction, and therefore something changeable and plastic. Yet how does this accord with the stereotypical pictures of young men and women presented above? This is a question that youth and school research has been struggling with during recent years. There is talk of changes, but also of persistent patterns. We will first look more closely at classroom research, and then gradually make our way out of the classroom.

There is a considerable amount of classroom research showing that boys, to a greater extent than girls, are favoured by and receive more attention from teachers (Öhrn 1991). The reasons boys receive more attention may vary. It may be because they are often viewed as troublesome and disobedient, but it may also be because they are seen as overachievers and as clear personalities. The downside of this is that girls tend to become invisible.

During the 1990s these patterns changed in a clear way. Educational research shows that girls generally out-perform boys. Today, for example, women constitute the majority of all individuals continuing to higher education. Naturally, this is also reflected in changed patterns of interaction in the classroom. For instance, Öhrn (2000) showed at the beginning of the 1990s that some previously irrefutable sex differences seemed to be giving way. She was able to show that, in several of the ninth-grade classes she studied, there was a great deal of evidence indicating that young women had the upper hand in the classroom and also had the most contact with teachers. At the time, this was a sensational finding. People were used to reading that young men predominated and received the most attention in the classroom, which was actually the case in several of the classes Öhrn studied.

One interesting finding from Öhrn's study is that girls in the girl-dominated classes were often described as a group or a gang. There was sometimes talk of a Girl Mafia. On the other hand, teachers found it difficult to differentiate among the girls and, thus, to see them as individuals. Boys, however, were often visible as individuals, sometimes owing precisely to their personalities.

The changes described by different researchers have been met with considerable attention, and discussions have been pursued concerning the cause of poor school performance among boys. Other authors, however, consider that there is a tendency to exaggerate these changes. Young women have certainly improved their school performance in certain respects. But the fact remains that, with time, it is still men who procure the most prestigious positions and the best-paid jobs in society (Connell 2000; Francis and Skelton 2001; Öhrn 2002).

We may establish at this point that the picture of young women as passive, subordinated, shy and invisible has partly been played out. A number of empirical studies instead depict young women who are active, forward looking, independent and high performing (Paecter 2000). In her study of a girl-dominated class, Öhrn shows how the young women actively took over the role of teacher. This concerned a class in which some racism could be observed. The teacher dismissed the notion completely, saying that it was just a trend among the boys that would soon blow over. But a gang of young women in the class took the situation more seriously. They became actively involved in trying to counteract racism. When the girls wanted time off from class to participate in an anti-racism demonstration, the boys and the teacher were opposed. What is most remarkable here is the alliance formed between the teacher and the boys. The girls did succeed, however, in pointing out shortcomings in how the school dealt with this particular issue.

At the same time as young women assert themselves and become involved in issues of justice, a picture is emerging of young men as underachievers, passive and alienated. Moreover, young men are often viewed as potential criminals, violent and generally problematic.

Thus, it seems we may establish that the balance between the sexes has changed somewhat. Young women have improved their school performance in many respects. They have become more active and visible. But this does not mean that the performance of young men has generally declined. To understand these new patterns, we must study the connections between class, gender and ethnicity. Some scholars consider that this is primarily a matter of class patterns. The underachieving young men are found among the working class, while the new young women belong mainly to the middle class.

The most recent studies seem to show that we are dealing with a more complicated classroom situation. In her survey of Scandinavian as well as some Anglo-Saxon classroom research, Öhrn (2000) shows how several studies have helped to nuance the previously predominant and stereotypical picture of gender in schools. She also establishes that these studies reveal many results that are contradictory and difficult to interpret. At the same time as certain shifts in the power balance are occurring, we can also discern how young men continue to control and dominate young women. This is taking place not least through sexual dominance.

In a Swedish study of sex education at one high school, we see how a teacher tries to counteract students' various preconceptions about homosexuality, gender and sexuality. We also gain insight into how the students themselves feel about and relate to these questions (Bäckman 2003). Eva, the fictitious name given to the teacher, tries in different ways – for example through value-judgement exercises and showing films – to create a broader understanding of, for example, the situation of homosexuals. This is anything but easy. The students who react most negatively are, of course, the young men. At one point, one of them bursts out with the following tirade: 'Are we gonna see a film about fags!? Then I'm going home!' (Bäckman 2003: 79). On another occasion, a gang of young men pretend to vomit and ceaselessly throw out comments. Thus it appears to be relatively difficult to work with this type of question. On the other hand, Bäckman establishes that the teacher does seem to have succeeded in her mission. In the end, the young men back down from their categorical repudiation and develop a more nuanced outlook.

Although this teacher is doing her best to create scope for a more nuanced and liberal view on sexuality, the students find it relatively difficult to take in the subject matter. Bäckman shows how these young people tend to reproduce classic gender patterns. This concerns, for example, how the picture of a sexually active young woman is negatively charged, while young men are given more latitude for their sexuality. Similarly, young women who masturbate are viewed as disgusting, while young men are reserved the right to different means of sexual expression. Although Eva works hard to call into question many conventional conceptions of gender and sexuality, it seems that the young people's everyday reality and understandings are largely just the opposite of this liberal outlook on sexuality. On the other hand, Bäckman seems to have found certain tendencies towards change and towards disintegration of these gender patterns. Generally, however, this study reveals a picture of a rather slow-moving sexual sphere.

Our ambition is to use material from different current investigations of young people's sexuality to show that their construction of gender and sexuality is actually very complex and difficult to interpret. Sexuality is largely a matter of power, boundaries and control. But it is, naturally, also about desire, longing and love. Many of the studies of young people's sexuality in and outside school have provided support for the notion that young men and women live in separate worlds or in different cultural realities. The purpose of our book is to use existing Scandinavian and Anglo-Saxon research to discuss and fill out this picture.

Gender Paradoxes

The existing research on youth, school, gender and sexuality presents a contradictory picture of the situation today. Scandinavian as well as Anglo-Saxon findings show that many of the typical gender patterns have been maintained over time. But here we are not speaking of total stability and lack of change, but instead of relative and slow change. Boundaries are being moved and shifted. Above all, we find solid empirical support for the claim that young women have moved their positions forward and that young men have taken more ambivalent positions. There are also some studies indicating that a rather widespread change is taking place today in how young men see themselves and in how they view questions of equality, intimacy and masculine identity.

By way of conclusion, we will look more closely at how gender is reproduced with respect to three different areas and principles.

1. *Performance.* Young women are performing better and better in school and are increasingly likely to continue to higher education. On the other hand, in several European countries, we see that young men are tending to fall behind. This has been discussed extensively in certain countries. There is great concern about the

fact that young men's academic performance is declining. On the other hand, several of the scholars we have referenced consider that discussions on men losing their position are characterized by great exaggeration. For instance, it is still the case that men generally dominate academia. This is particularly evident if we look at the proportions of men and women who are leading researchers and professors. Moreover, many scholars point out the great differences in performance between men from different social classes. Careful analysis shows that poor academic performance is seen particularly in working-class men.

2. *Choice of subject/labour market.* School subjects are often viewed on the basis of how they are charged with respect to gender. Thus, some subjects are seen as feminine and others as masculine. In certain subjects, teachers even divide the class on the basis of gender. This tends to be the case in, for example, physical education. Just as school subjects are charged with meaning on the basis of gender, we can also see how the labour market is marked by a high degree of gender-based segregation. Among the European countries, Sweden's labour market shows extreme gender-based segregation. There is, thus, a strong association between what you do, like and work with and who you are. This is largely a question of status and power. It is considered unmanly to like certain school subjects and to have certain types of occupations.

3. *Sexuality/sphere of intimacy.* Although great changes in the sphere of intimacy are taking place today, hierarchical gender patterns are also still being reproduced and maintained over time. The construction of gender is intimately interwoven with how we view sexuality. In this way, sexuality is also largely a question of power. Many of the studies referenced here show that a considerable number of the boundaries drawn between the genders concern outlooks on sexuality. Men who are viewed as feminine or homosexual are disparaged and, if it comes to the worst, subjected to violence. This also implies that many stereotypical attitudes toward manly sexuality are being reproduced. There is a tendency to present male sexuality as unproblematic and uncomplicated – a picture in rather poor accordance with men's own experiences. At the same time, there is an ongoing and constant struggle to establish new ways to look at gender in order to transcend rigid boundaries and to promote equality. This struggle is manifested in many different ways. In this context, we find that more and more men are becoming involved in these issues.

In this chapter we have focused on the schools, the classroom and how everyday interactions between young men and women are formed and given shape. In a time when male power is being questioned and destabilized, there are naturally countless attempts to maintain and reinforce this power. This may be manifested in many ways. We have tried to show how changes in the academic sphere of the schools are clearly tied to questions of gender and sexuality. In the subsequent chapter, we will leave the world of schools and direct our attention to how different groupings of young people develop particular attitudes towards the body, sexuality, desire and identity.

Chapter 4

Gender and Sexuality in Youth Culture Research

Educational research has largely focused on teachers' relations to and images of students. This implies concentration on performance, curricula, teaching and students. To find studies on how young people interact with and relate to one another outside the classroom, we must also look to other disciplines. When we look at studies of how junior high or high school students construct their gender identities, it is striking how much of this process concerns sexuality. The demarcations, categorizations and definitions that young people make are often based on relatively prejudiced outlooks on sexuality. This is probably clearest among young men.

This chapter deals with and focuses on how youth research has contributed to different ways of constructing and gender young people. The purpose of this presentation is to develop a background to the study that will be presented in the next part of the book, partly to situate this study in a research field, and partly to use the images and interpretations done in the 1970s to 1990s as a contrast to our study.

We begin by considering a fictional contribution to the discussion on young masculinity, in order to provide the reader with a picture of this masculinity that is complex, multifaceted and hopeful. This will serve as a contrast to the great amount of research findings presenting another, more stereotyped picture.

At the beginning of the 1980s, Swedish author Sven Lindqvist published his autobiographical book *En älskares dagbok* (*A Lover's Diary*, 1981). This is a penetrating and courageous account of young male inability and of fragile sexuality. In Lindqvist's book we find no self-confident, potent, daring and absolute masculinity. He writes in a tender and beautiful way about one young man's fears. At the beginning of the book, a young man, Sven, is courting a young woman, Gerd. Both of these teenagers are out taking a long walk. After a while, Sven begins to wonder if he should dare to kiss Gerd. But he is obsessed by doubt about his abilities. Moreover, he is afraid she will reject him. The walk is taking a long time and it is soon time to say goodbye. Gerd sighs and says it is time to go back. Sven follows her to the gate. They say goodbye. Lindqvist writes: 'I saw her eyes, her soft smile in the porch light. My head spun. Why hadn't I dared? Why was I such a goddamned, hopeless, crazy, foolish idiot who was always failing at everything? Why?' (Lindqvist 1981: 21; my translation). Sven's self-contempt is flowing freely. His failure is complete. Following this are several other accounts of his awkward attempts to bring about a moment of love. Somewhat later in the book, we find a situation in which Sven and another young woman, Emmeli, are at home alone. This is the first night they sleep together. There are no contraceptives available, so there can be no sex. Yet sleeping together, completely naked, was fantastic. Sven stopped doubting his own worth and was able to fight against his constant, nagging lack of faith in himself as a man. At their next meeting, Sven is prepared. He has purchased condoms. Here is a brief passage from the book:

> Of course it came back, the next time. I had bought condoms. But I was too nervous and couldn't keep stiff long enough to get one on. Emmeli was disappointed and she showed it. So we only tried once. The disgrace was too great, the fear of failure was too great. (Lindqvist 1981: 62; my translation)

In his book, Lindqvist succeeds in depicting male inability, insufficiency and fear of failure with great care and tenderness. It is a beautiful portrait of one young man's complicated emotional path through life. In many respects, this story runs counter to much of what is written about young men, perhaps particularly in the public debate.

We might say that Lindqvist was ahead of his time. Today much more is happening. There is a growing body of literature and research focused on young men. In our neighbouring country, Denmark, a book entitled *Pikstormerne* (2000; the title translates as *Cock Raiders*) was published, edited by men's studies scholar Niels Ulrik Sörensen. Here we find ten essays on young masculinity. This is a book that challenges our conventional ideas about masculinity and that breaks new ground. The essays present portraits of young masculinity that stress insecurity, a new orientation and a willingness to break with traditional masculinity. We will return to these tendencies later, after the following section on the relation between masculinity, identity and power.

The following is a brief summary of some of the research on young masculinity. Much of this work has focused on how young men relate to one another and to young women. How do they define the boundary between what is manly and unmanly? How do they view 'the feminine'? In what way is ethnicity drawn into the construction of masculinity? And finally, how is all of this charged with sexual content?

Male fellowship may be discussed and analysed in terms of *homosociality*. This form of sociality constitutes a mixture of a desire for intimacy, strictly regulated group solidarity and a need for maintaining fixed boundaries in relation to the surrounding world. The purpose of this is to keep the group together and to create a strong feeling of collectivity. This apparently strong male fellowship originates both in a longing for and in a fear of intimacy, and is characterized by, for example considerable homophobia. Hugs, kisses and other intimate behaviours are enveloped in careful rules and in norms concerning what is appropriate. Physical closeness and the type of intimacy that often seem so natural for women are allowed in sports arenas, on certain festive occasions and at, for example a stag party, when the man is about to leave his inner circle of male friends (Andreasson 2003).

The intimate is generally associated with the 'feminine' and different. Homosociality, thus, constitutes an effective barrier against women and against what is viewed as 'the feminine'. In this way, homosociality is a paradox: Its purpose is to create intimacy and solidarity, but at the same time young men are coming together and forming a wall of defence against everything that is considered feminine.

In his classic study of how young men are socialized into masculinity, British scholar Paul Willis shows how contempt for the other helps to keep the group together. The teenage working-class boys under study revolt against the middle-class school culture. This revolt involves not only a struggle against the predominant culture at the school, but also the development of a fragile feeling of superiority. We have chosen an excerpt from Willis's book that mirrors these young men's construction of boundaries in relation to the other.

PW: […] Why not be like the ear'oles, why not try and get CSEs?
—: They don't get any fun, do they?
Derek: Cos they'm prats like, one kid he's got on his report now, he's got five As and one B.
—: Who's that?
Derek: Birchall.
Spanksy: I mean, what will they remember of their school life? What will they have to look back on? Sitting in a classroom, sweating their bollocks off, you know, while we've been … I mean look at the things we can look back on, fighting the Pakis, fighting on the Jas [i.e. Jamaicans]. Some of the things we've done on teachers, it'll be a laff when we look back on it. (Willis 1977:14)

Here we see, in a condensed form, how the young men are trying to construct a convincing identity. The geeks and the teachers are used to symbolize the middle-class school culture. Through jokes, sarcasm and mischief, the boys transform the legitimate school culture into something non-desirable and reprehensible. Group solidarity and male identity are created at the cost of respect for teachers, geeks, immigrants and women. When the young men use the word 'cunt', they also place themselves in a highly sexist gender order in which this name for the female genitalia is used to show contempt for the geeks' unmanly behaviour. Thus, designations for the feminine are used to indicate what 'the lads' do not wish to be.

Nothing is allowed to threaten this male fellowship. The greatest threat to this form of intimacy is constituted by the young men's increasingly frequent dealings with the opposite sex. Girls can never be fully-fledged members of these groups of young men. They are viewed as occasional guests and, as such, are also granted only peripheral positions in the gang. In Máirtín Mac an Ghaill's study of school youth, this pattern emerges with considerable clarity. The following is an excerpt from one of his many group discussions with teenage boys:

Noel: On the first instinct you're interested in looks, then other things later on, like having a laugh. You're with your girl and you think she's like a pot of gold. Like my mates are jealous of me with my girlfriend and she keeps on at me about them. Sometimes it's difficult to keep everyone happy.
Stephen: When you're trying to pick a girl up, then yes, if you're out with your mates, you would spend more time with her to chat her up. But if she's a more regular

M.M.:	girlfriend and you're out with her and your mates come in, yes you would spend more time with them and she would go into the background.

M.M.:   Why is that?

Wayne: It's just normal. Girls are important but a particular girl isn't going to be around long is she? You always come back to your mates in the end, don't you?

M.M.:   What do young women think?

William: Some accept it. Others are unreasonable and go off moaning, which just shows you we're better off without her.

M.M.:   Don't you think it's fair they act like that?

Stephen: Most girls know the score, the others will only give you trouble, believe me. (Mac an Gaill 1997: 105)

Although far from all mixed-sex group constellations are of this nature, the pattern does recur in several different investigations of boys' and youth gangs. Girls who protest against this male dominance are viewed as deviant and problematic. For the young men Mac an Ghaill studied, girls only complicated their otherwise rather simple joint existence. Their male fellowship was idealized and presented as an oasis of trust and mutual friendship.

The connection that was elucidated by Paul Willis, between subcultures consisting only of men and sexism and racism is also revealed in Les Back's study of young people in the Docklands of London. What is viewed as manly and unmanly varies. For example, Back finds that strong ties between young white and black men sometimes develop, whereas young Vietnamese men are defined as belonging outside the male fellowship and are viewed as unmanly. This is made clear in Les Back's interview with Chas:

We passed a Vietnamese refugee and her son walking back from a shopping excursion. Chas turned, 'There is one thing though – I can't stand the chinks. Their cooking stinks and they keep themselves to themselves like. They don't want to mix.' I asked 'But isn't that just as bad as saying that all black people are muggers.' He replied, 'Na! That's not the same at all! My black mates wouldn't let people walk over them the way Vietnamese people do – do you know what I mean? Black people have nuff respect for who they are. If you said things to dem you'd get nuff licks (physical retribution).' (Back 1996: 69)

Young Vietnamese men are placed in the category of the unmanly, because they have not succeeded in developing the clearly masculine codes prevalent in this lower-class urban culture – a culture in which being indistinct and gentle natured is associated with a lack of masculine traits and attributes. These young men's group solidarity is resting on a highly fragile foundation. By creating rigid distinctions between themselves and others – such that the *in-group* is seen as manly, loyal and is subjected to unconditional idealization and the *out-group* is left to symbolize everything that is weak, indistinct and worthless – these young men develop inflexible and in many respects dysfunctional identities.

It is often the case that strong sexualization is attached to men who are seen as weak, feminine and unworthy, thus as unmanly and 'fagish'. The male hierarchy is upheld through violence and oppression. Sexuality is drawn into this game, and it is here stereotypes are created that distinguish the manly world – which is potent, sexually active and in control – from the feminine world – which is charged with weakness, passivity and subordination.

A number of British studies have revealed a widespread contempt for and repudiation of homosexual men. This contempt and its associated violence also affect heterosexual men who move in circles that are seen as homosexual. The following is an excerpt from Rob and Pam Gilbert's study of teenage boys in an Australian school:

Peter: I don't understand why I deserve to be bashed for who I was. The ironic thing about this is that the offenders were only working on the presumption that I was gay. They didn't know for a fact that I was as I didn't either at that stage of my life.

Marcus: Even though I eventually realized that I was gay, a few of the outcasts I became friends with did not and were heterosexual. They suffered the same degradation because they were different in various shapes and forms. (Gilbert and Gilbert 1998: 162)

The Gilberts' study shows how contempt for homosexual, feminine and otherwise different men is interwoven with views on school and even on particular school subjects. For instance, one common opinion concerned the subject of English. The young men did not like this subject. According to them, only girls and fags like this kind of 'feminine' subject. Thus, we see here how even school subjects are categorized and placed on a continuum of degree of masculinity.

Much of the existing research on young men presents a rather rigid and absolute masculinity. There is not a great deal of room here for the weaknesses and fragility shown by Sven Lindqvist. This is probably related to some extent to scholars' interests in analysing male power patterns. Yet it is also related to a social reality. We will conclude this section by pointing out a number of tendencies toward change and possible constructions of contemporary young masculinity. Later on in the book, we will use new research findings to develop these lines of argument.

During the 1990s, there was a notable increased interest in studying young men. This is partly the result of influences from critical men's studies and partly an effect of discussions concerning young men's declining school performance. A good deal has been written about these issues, above all in England (see, for example Connell 2000; O'Donnell and Sharpe 2000; Frosh et al 2002). This body of literature has tried to nuance the picture of young masculinity in various ways. At the same time, empirical studies show that many of the patterns established in previous research still remain. Thus, the picture emerging here is rather contradictory. The aim of many scholars is to identify tendencies toward change, yet the data they collect still portray a situation in which many 'old' patterns persist.

We may establish, then, that researchers tend to depict and thereby to reproduce more general patterns. What is lacking, however, are studies of alternative masculinities, for example of young feminist men (Johansson 2005). As we move away from more general male patterns, reactions and attitudes and toward special groups, we can study another picture of young masculinity. Here we find active resistance to sexism and homophobia. General patterns notwithstanding, today there is a considerable group of young men who have a more nuanced outlook on sexuality and gender. In one major Swedish survey study of young people's sexuality, which we will discuss further in the next chapter, it is shown that a relatively large proportion of young men – though not the majority – have a positive attitude toward homosexuality. The same study also supports the notion that young people today have developed a more liberal attitude towards questions concerning love and sexuality. What emerges in particular is a picture of a more active and pleasure-affirming young woman (Johansson 2005).

Feminist Resistance

> It is not the case that girls do too much when they are too young, but instead that they have the opportunity to do too little too late. To the extent that all-female subcultures – in which the gang comes first – are able to check these processes and offer their members a collective self-confidence that exceeds their need for 'boys', such a development would entail a significant advancement in the area of youth culture policies. (McRobbie 1989: 128)

Feminist criticism of British subculture research led, among other things, to a number of concrete studies of young women's social and cultural reality (McRobbie and Garber 1986). In male subcultures, such as motorcycle gangs and other male groupings, women often play a peripheral role. There are no self-evident and independent female positions. Here, young women must be satisfied with serving as helpers or, if it comes to the worst, as aesthetic features of an otherwise male-dominated culture. In several other subcultures, for example the mods and hippies, women have a more prominent position. In androgynous subcultures, young women participate on equal terms; they help to form the culture and 'the feminine' is highly valued. Also observed in these cultures, however, are tendencies towards assigning young women to subordinated or idealized positions.

While boys learn to master the public arena, girls learn to fear it. Girls learn to dress in such a way as to not arouse the sexual interest of men. Furthermore, they learn to accept that they cannot stay out too late at pubs and dance clubs, at least not without a male companion, and to be careful in their contacts with unknown men. Girls learn these things for their own safety, so that they will not be accosted by men who have no respect for women's personal boundaries. If young women internalize this type of sexual threat and shape their lifestyles according to this threat to a great degree, they risk the loss of their own freedom. In the worst case, this type of socialization may lead to *internalized sexism*, that is, that young women accept certain kinds of repressive definitions of their own sex (Holland et al 1998). How this form of self-repression functions is clearly shown in the following excerpt from Christine Griffin's classic study of young women:

Cathy: I think that girls who get out in slit skirts, and minis like, they deserve it. They're asking for it.

CG: Would you go out in a mini?

Cathy: Oh yeh sometimes.

CG: If you were attacked, would you think it was your fault?

Cathy: Oh no course not. (Griffin 1985: 6)

By talking negatively about certain clothing styles, Cathy partly concedes to the sexist division of young women into the morally reprehensible and the conscientious and, in this way, she helps to reproduce a repressive gender order. Another way to handle this situation is to withdraw, to create intimate oases to which young men have no access and where young women are able to cultivate a certain type of rationality and relational orientation.

There is a close connection between young women's aesthetic orientation and their cultivation of intimate relations. While they devote themselves to clothes, fashion and other aesthetic activities, an intimate space is created that lends itself to discussions of relations, feelings, romantic dreams and existential problems. In the small, intimate environment of the fitting room, a specific kind of rationality and group culture are created. The cramped fitting room constitutes a contrast to the public arena that is mastered by young and grown men.

> Not only clothes are dealt with in the fitting room, but also relationships to parents, love and appearance complexes. Girls comfort one another: 'your thighs aren't fat, look at mine!' They give one another good advice: 'you can talk to your mom about it sometime when she's in a good mood.' They give support: 'Of course he likes you. You're so pretty!' This relational work on which girls' same-sex friend culture rests blossoms luxuriantly in the greenhouse that the fitting room represents. (Ganetz 1992: 92)

The fitting room and other spheres of intimacy function as bases for cultivation of a certain type of conversation – one focused on relational work. The knowledge and form of reflexivity emerging from this work – often called *the rationality of caring* – contrast sharply with young men's end–means rationality. A number of Swedish studies of young people's lifestyles have shown that young men are more likely to cultivate distinct lifestyles and subcultures than are young women (Johansson and Miegel 1992). These results, however, may be partly a consequence of choice of methods and an insufficient analysis. For instance, it is possible that young women are more likely to combine different styles, be less orthodox and accept diversity and breach of style than are young men. Helena Wulff's study of around 20 young English women points in this direction. The description of Doris provides a good example of how this may be manifested in a specific case.

> Neither did Doris seem to be all that much into the style, or styles – she actually mentioned two – that she said were hers: Skinhead and New Romantic. Clearly she liked their respective forms of music, but she did not mind having black friends at the club, nor did she have a crew cut or wear Skinhead clothes. And she did not dress in frill blouses or have her hair brushed back in a beehive, in line with what was supposed to be the typical

attributes of a New Romantic girl. Doris claimed that her mood determined which youth style she chose: 'If it's a bad day I'm a Skinhead, if it's a good I'm New Romantic'. (Wulff 1988: 102)

Doris's mood determines which style she will adopt on any given day. She combines styles without considering any cultural rules. Although she does not sympathize with the Skinheads, she uses symbols and codes taken directly from that subculture. We see here a lack of the striving for system and coherence that sometimes characterizes young men's lifestyles. While young men's styles are made visible in the public arena, young women's more complicated, but also less distinct styles are subject to marginalization. The question is, however, whether this picture is actually correct.

Elisabet Öhrn's study of girls' influence in schools shows a pattern partly different from that revealed by studies showing *friend dyads* to be a typical pattern of organization among young women. In the classroom it is the girls who dominate, who organize resistance to aspects of the teachers' instruction and who react to injustices.

Jakob:	It's usually a couple of them who start protesting at once. Who agree there's something wrong.
Donald:	Yeah, it's mostly girls that like protest. Then the others start, start to bring up things and stuff.
Jakob:	Well, they're good ... Girls are good at catching on to things like. If one girl thinks something is wrong, it's like 'Right, I think so too' like. (Öhrn 1998: 32)

Elisabet Öhrn puts forward the idea that the gang of girls constitutes the basis of collective mobilization. This would seem to indicate that young women learn to take advantage of intimate relations in advancing their own causes and in making themselves heard. There is a great deal of evidence to support the observation that young women are beginning to conquer the public sphere and, thereby, to compete with young men on increasingly equal terms.

One important theme in the research on young women concerns resistance strategies. Sue Lees (1993) differentiates three different reactions to repression:

1. *Resistance.* One approach is to combat young men's attempts at depreciating and condescending to the opposite sex and to put up an active resistance. The Riot Grrls movement is one extreme example of this strategy. Using symbolic transformations, many of the sexist expressions produced by young men may be changed into resistance. For instance, it is possible to transform the word cunt, which is often used condescendingly, into something positive and powerful. In this way, young women take back the initiative in defining sexual terms and in determining how we relate to the female gender.
2. *Resignation.* Here, young women give up and conform. They tend to defend their young men and develop an outlook in which young men's behaviour is viewed as natural and in which they let 'the man in their heads' control their own self-reflection. By taking on male attributes and behaviours, these young women adapt to the gender order.

3. *Avoidance.* By downplaying their own sexuality and avoiding exposing themselves to young men's sexual challenges, some young women are able to maintain their self-esteem, though in a phobic manner.

If resistance only constitutes some variation within the framework of an otherwise relatively fixed template – in this case the male-dominated society – all investigations will tend to lead us in the same direction. Is it possible to conceive of any form of sexuality that exists outside this power structure? It must be possible to talk about *reflexive-free zones*, in which much of the ordinary power game is turned upside down or even knocked over. This structural power cannot permeate all situations in everyday life.

A Theoretical Position

The research discussed here has its roots in women's studies and gender studies. This implies a point of departure from lines of thought concerning power and gender. As we have seen, there is much evidence to say that the classic gender patterns of male superordination and female subordination still remain. On the other hand, several recent studies show that a great deal of change has actually taken place. This change is perhaps most evident in studies of young women.

According to Robert Connell (1995), masculinity is stratified and differentiated partly in relation to a *gender order*, a situation of male dominance. At the same time a *class and status dimension* runs through and complicates this hierarchy. The concept of hegemony suggests that the importance of masculine and feminine is constantly open to negotiations and shifts in meaning. These negotiations result in a *gender order* in which men are superordinate and women subordinate. But this order is not static. A struggle for power is underway concerning how the boundaries are to be drawn. Positions change and gender is redefined.

Dominant masculinity is tied to societal institutions and central spheres of power, such as industry and the state. Yet this does not imply that the ideals created are static. Today, classic career masculinity – in which men deny themselves home, household and children – is being questioned. Instead, new demands are being made with regard to fatherhood and childcare. Hegemonic masculinity is being renegotiated. However, masculinity is still largely associated with career, power and strength. New ideals have a hard time gaining ground.

Using the concepts *complicity* and *subordination*, Connell shows how men are forced in many ways to relate to male dominance. *Complicity* means that men, by concurring in and making use of the advantages of this dominance, display their strong relationship to hegemony. I have added to the model the concept of *negotiation* to enable representation of the complexity of the situation. I consider that many men are actually trying to change their positions and, for example, to develop a modern form of fatherhood.

The position *subordination* marks alienation and that which is viewed as unmanly. This may concern homosexuals, for example, or men who are for some reason defined as 'feminine'. I have added two more positions to Connell's model: an *oppositional* and a *nostalgic* position. *Oppositional* implies that criticism is being directed at dominant masculinity (T. Johansson 2000). Much of the work done within male networks and other critical men's organizations may be placed here. *Nostalgic* implies the defence of traditional male ideals. This often has to do with a longing to return to a time in which masculinity was not constantly being threatened. A good deal of the Anglo-Saxon discussion on good fathers tends to end up in this position. The concern here, thus, is not to develop equality between mothers and fathers, but to safeguard old cultural ideals in which men and women perform different tasks and have different responsibilities.

These different positions may also be held by women. For instance, it is conceivable that some women come near or even hold the hegemonic-dominant position. This is, after all, a structural order. Similarly, we can imagine that both men and women negotiate about how work and power in the home should be divided. If we consider that men and women may hold different positions in the social space represented in the model, then we can use the model to discuss issues of power, gender and sexuality more generally.

The research findings discussed in this chapter may be taken as support for the notion that we still find ourselves within the framework of a system of male dominance – if you wish, a societal patriarchy. At the same time, we are able to observe a number of tendencies towards change. This means that, in terms of percentages, we find most women in a subordinate, negotiating or oppositional position and most men in a hegemonic, complicit or nostalgic position. But we may also find certain men who could be placed in an oppositional position and, likewise, women who could be placed in a nostalgic position. Thus, it is important to consider that, at the level of the individual, it is possible to move between any of the different positions in the model.

If we use this model as our point of departure, we can imagine the formation of coalitions between men and women. This way of thinking also implies gradual changes and shifts in the meanings of masculine hegemony and in how it is charged. As more and more women take on positions of power, such changes would seem to be particularly likely.

The research discussed here seems to indicate that the gender patterns that emerge and are created outside and in the schools are characterized by a certain degree of change. Today we see constant criticism of masculine hegemony. Such criticism may be manifested in different ways. In this chapter we have considered some of these manifestations, but there are, of course, other examples of resistance.

In the next section of this book we will use material from the Swedish study in order to develop the perspectives and findings discussed in this part of the book.

PART III
Desire and Identity
in Contemporary Sweden

Chapter 5

Gender Order or Disorder?

with Nils Hammarén

The Context

Sweden has often been viewed as a liberal country in terms of its sexual values, including a rational and liberal view of the body and sexual variation. Swedish studies show that young people today are quite open-minded with regard to sex. One-night stands have increased, young people have sex with more partners and differences between the sexes have decreased (Herlitz 2001). The study presented in this chapter also validates this picture. However, this particular study also confirms, in some respects, a gender-stereotyped picture, especially with regard to homosexuality and pornography.

Much of the research conducted in the 1970s and 1980s on youth, gender and sexuality presents the polarized patterns discussed in the previous chapters. The picture changed somewhat during the 1990s, particularly in the latter part of that decade. What we see among today's scholars is an increasing desire to highlight phenomena that complicate this picture. One reason for this may be found in the changed theoretical influences. A poststructuralist theoretical framework challenges researchers to seek out the cracks, shifts and ambivalences discernible in the gender order (Butler 1990). This involves deconstructing prevailing conceptions and elucidating processes and potentials for change. Such a search includes clear Utopian possibilities. Yet it is still important to maintain focus on issues of justice and power.

The empirical foundation upon which this chapter is based derives from an extensive Swedish survey study conducted in 2000–2001 in two Swedish cities – Gothenburg and Kalmar. In this chapter, we have chosen to present only the results from the surveys completed in the high schools (650 surveys). This age group was chosen because it better matches the age groups found in the other qualitative studies that together form the basis of our continued line of argument. Thus, the young participants in the study were in the age range 17–18 years and attended high school when the survey study was conducted. The participating high schools were chosen to reflect, as far as possible, the distribution between the sexes and between young people enrolled in vocational versus theoretical programmes.[1]

---

1 However, in the next chapter we will use the material from the whole survey.

To facilitate readability, we have chosen to avoid using too many tables. The statistics used are also relatively simple, including percentages and simple tests of significance. Our purpose is primarily to show tendencies and some of the variation found in the data.

The data and the conclusions drawn in this chapter are based on a more extensive Swedish dataset. The question is: to what extent is it possible to generalize the results? We are able to establish that many of the most general patterns and tendencies towards change described and analysed in the book are also found in the Anglo-Saxon literature. Thus, in the West, general changes in sexuality and intimacy among young people seem to be taking place. Moreover, these tendencies are found both in empirical studies and in more theoretical discussions. We also find the same discussions in literature from, for example Latin America (Olvivaria 2003). It must be pointed out, however, that attitudes do vary across countries and different parts of the world. Sometimes such differences are relatively great and crucial. Also, a number of other factors play a role here – factors such as religion, ethnicity, GNP and politics. The question of the potential to generalize can only be addressed using a larger, comparative study. It is our hope that the present investigation will inspire such an effort.

The sexual landscape is in transformation. The gender stereotyped picture that still appears most frequently in youth research – and in certain feminist literature – must clearly be contested and revised. It is not our opinion that we have reached a point at which we may talk about gender equality, but we do feel it is necessary to deal with the complexity that is a result of late-modern developments. Reading Simone de Beauvoir is still worthwhile, but only through the lens of a contemporary view on the changing cultural landscape.

This chapter is organized in the following way: we first discuss the relation between romantic love and sexuality, then follows a section on how young people view homosexuality. Finally, we discuss the body and physical appearance. In the next chapter we will deal more thoroughly with the question of hegemonic masculinity and pornography.

Crossing Boundaries?

> The clitoris is the best part of the body. It is okay to gaze at and enjoy other people's bodies. Masturbation is a pleasant preoccupation. Menstruation is a sign of health and blood dripping down the legs is fantastic. Sex is breathtaking, raw and great whenever it happens. Our bodies give us more options than just a simple money-shot. We have endless desires and we know how to satisfy ourselves. (L. Johansson 2000: 34)

Contemporary young people shape their identity and sexuality in a complex and contradictory cultural landscape (Giddens 1992; Bauman 1999). Although the liberal view on sexuality has a strong influence on young people's attitudes and actions, this does not mean 'anything goes'. On the contrary, sexuality is still an area in which there are rules, norms and regulations. As Foucault (1978) has shown, the type and nature of the rules and regulations are changing all the time. In order to read young people's construction of sexuality, we must understand the relation between fields of knowledge, types of normativity and forms of subjectivity.

The romantic love complex is still a dominant cultural *Gestalt* (Giddens 1992; Frisell 1996). The individual holds a strong position in romantic love, constantly asking: 'Who am I?', 'What do I want in life?', 'What is happiness?' and so on. On the basis of these questions, romantic love has been successively transformed into the late-modern love relationship. It is no longer a question of finding a specific person, but of developing a specific relationship based on mutual respect, open discussions and equality. Thus, we are observing the gradual and slow erosion of romantic love.

The empirical material in our survey shows that the romantic love complex is gradually losing ground (Hammarén and Johansson 2002, 2005). A majority of the young participants accept that young women and men have sex with people they are not in love with. Young women are not seen in a different light to young men. However, the degree of acceptance of this kind of free sexual behaviour is lower among the younger participants (the 15-year-olds). At the same time, it does seem to be generally accepted that young people have one-night stands. Yet when we look more closely at this matter, the picture becomes increasingly complex.

There is a tenuous boundary between 'good' and 'bad' sexuality. Young people who have many sexual encounters are regarded with suspicion. Young women are generally under more pressure to behave correctly. Yet the view of the morally lacking young woman is clearly being contested. This was vividly expressed in one of our interviews:

Is a boy who has been having sex with many partners cool or attractive?
Abbas: No!
Ali: Maybe he's good at certain things, you know, like getting laid. But he doesn't have other abilities, like maintaining a relationship.
Sid: A player, he's a really bad character. I don't think any girl would want to go out with a player.

Whereas young women easily acquire bad reputations, young men still have a wider range of sexual opportunities. But young people are increasingly aware of the fact that young men and women are treated differently. The traditional image of the man who is in control and who takes the sexual initiative is changing. Our study shows that young people support and work for a more active female position. Women are no longer regarded as the weak or passive sex. As one of our male respondents expressed it:

Sebastian: Before, the boys were expected to take the initiative. But nowadays this has clearly changed. Girls are more active and boys are too shy.
So the girls make the first move more often?
Linda: Yeah, that's the way it works.
Sebastian: Yes, I agree.

The majority of the young people in our study agree with the statement that young women's need for sexuality is as great as young men's (Hammarén and Johansson

Table 5.1   'Girls should take the sexual initiative as often as boys do'

	Agree completely	Agree strongly	Agree partly	Agree a little	Disagree completely
Men (n=288)	59.7%	18.4%	16.0%	3.5%	2.4%
Women (n=347)	57.9%	21.3%	15.9%	2.6%	2.3%

Chi-2: 0.88

2002). Young women are not created exclusively in the male gaze. Female lust and desire are accepted and regarded as equal in value to male lust and desire. However, it must be stressed that we are using empirical material collected from statistical inquiries and qualitative interviews. How these ideals and attitudes are actually transformed and acted out in everyday life is a question for further ethnographic studies.

The romantic love complex is a major, predominant ideology in Western societies. This way of perceiving love and intimate relationships permeates the entire culture. When reading magazines, watching soap operas and different talk shows, it becomes obvious that romantic love is still a significant issue. At the same time, however, more liberal, individualistic ideals influence how people actually behave in everyday life.

One key finding from our survey is that young women generally express an active, lively view of sexuality. The passive, oppressed young woman found in the work of Beauvoir and others seems to have been replaced by a more active and competent female subject. This does not imply, of course, that we have seen the end of gender oppression.

This is shown clearly in Table 5.1, where we see that there are no direct gender differences at all with regard to attitudes toward young women taking the sexual initiative. We see that most of the young people in the study acknowledge female sexuality. Only a very small proportion of young people have negative attitudes toward young women actively affirming their own sexuality.

One of the main findings of our survey is that young people today are developing a resistance to traditional gender patterns. We see that young women use active strategies to deal with male dominance, and that young men condemn, to a certain extent, other young men's attitudes towards sexuality. Young people's sexuality is thus undergoing a process of change, whereby dual boundaries between gender roles are being modulated into a flexible mix of gender identities. Consequently, both young men's sexuality and young women's sexuality constitute a complex and sometimes inconsistent area of study.

One of the reasons for this complex situation is that youth sexuality is influenced by several contradictory discourses. Young people today express both conservative and subversive opinions. Liberal attitudes toward homosexuality share space with homophobia, the romantic love complex competes with a kind of plastic sexuality, and shame and shamelessness are interchangeable. Sexuality is therefore *liquid* and in constant motion, making it difficult to capture (Bauman 1999; Hammarén and Johansson 2001).

The gender identities of young men and women are also inconsistent. The traditional opinion that they inhabit different worlds with totally different sexualities and attitudes is currently changing into a more flexible view that emphasizes ambivalence and fissures. Young men's and young women's attitudes are converging in several arenas in society, at the same time as certain areas are still characterized by tendencies toward maintaining the traditional gender order. Homosexuality is one of these areas.

Homophobia and Ambivalence

During the past decade, the issue of homosexuality has been widely discussed and studied. Homosexual rights have increased and attitudes toward homosexuals have become more tolerant. The homosexual individual has also been made more visible. Homosexuals appear on television and in newspapers and magazines; there are Internet sites for the gay community and organizations representing homosexuals are increasing in number. Tolerance among young people has also increased rapidly over the past ten years (Herlitz 2001; Forsberg 2000).

Despite this development, young people today often feel ambivalence and insecurity when discussing homosexuality. There are still repressive tendencies, especially among young men. The kind of intimacy they develop with their peer group – *homosociality* – consists of a complex mix of a longing for intimacy (with strict regulations for body contact, however) and a need to maintain borders in relation to their surroundings. In this mix, homophobia is quite often present.

In one of our interviews, a young man expressed how he thought he would react if he found out his friend was gay.

Mansour: It would make me sick.
But would you dissociate yourself from him? He is your best friend.
Mansour: I would try to get him normal again. [...] I think they are twisted up here [in the head, our remark]. I think therapy would help.

Young men's intimacy usually includes more regulations than does young women's intimacy. Male fellowship is often structured by strict rules and homophobic tendencies. Homophobia is, however, not absent in young women's minds, although it is not expressed in the same way as in the peer group of young men. For example, Linda said 'I don't know what I'd have done if I'd realized I was a lesbian, I would have killed myself. No, but I think it's "ugh".' Here, homophobia becomes a strategy for defining oneself as 'normal' and 'okay', that is resistance facilitates the personal identity process (Henriksson and Lundahl 1993). Mac an Ghaill has tried to understand this inner logic of the psychic relations of domination:

Binarism operates in the same way as splitting and projection: the centre expels its anxieties, contradictions and irrationalities onto the subordinate term, filling it with the antithesis of its own identity; the Other, in its very alienness, simply mirrors and represents what is deeply familiar to the centre, but projected outside of itself. (Mac an Ghaill 1996: 94)

Table 5.2   'Homosexuals should be allowed to adopt children'

	Agree completely	Agree strongly	Agree partly	Agree a little	Disagree completely
Men (n=290)	19.3%	8.3%	12.8%	11.3%	48.3%
Women (n=350)	31.7%	16.9%	19.7%	9.7%	22.0%

Chi-2: 0.00

Our empirical survey data show that the young men expressed homophobic tendencies to a great extent (Hammarén and Johansson 2002). 26% of the young men and 10% of the young women agreed completely with the following statement: *Homosexuality is a mental illness.* On the other hand, 37% of the young men and 68% of the young women disagreed completely. Our study also shows that young women have more homosexual fantasies than do young men, and that young women were more likely to report becoming aroused when having homosexual fantasies. These results show the wide range of opinions about homosexuality. Traditionalism replaces subversion and vice versa.

When we look more closely at young people's attitudes toward homosexuality, we find great variation. First of all, we are able to establish that young men are generally more homophobic than are young women. For instance, young men are very hesitant about homosexuals adopting children. The results in Table 5.2 reveal a significant difference between young men and women with regard to this issue. Yet we should note that a relatively large proportion of young women also have negative attitudes towards homosexuals' right to adoption. Just as interesting as the significant gender differences, however, is the existence of considerable within-gender variation.

One way of understanding and explaining this dual gender order is to focus on attitudes toward homosexuality. Men state more often than do women that they grew up in surroundings full of prejudices toward homosexuals. The male homosexual is probably the more visible homosexual individual in society, and therefore also the most threatening (Nordenmark 2000). Because masculinity has long been equated with sexual power (over women), male homosexuality has become a threat to the social and sexual political order, and homophobia is intertwined with a traditional gender order (Lewin 1991). But why are women more tolerant? Could it be due to their experience as the subordinated sex? Can women, for this reason, more easily identify themselves with subordinated sexuality, as incarnated by the homosexual?

As we have mentioned earlier, it is important to note that many young men are positive toward homosexuality and that some young women are negative. Thus, what is emerging here is a complex picture. Explanations for this great variation may certainly be found in other factors such as class, ethnicity and lifestyle.

The Body

In discussions with young people about physical appearance, bodies and the partner ideal, questions often emerge concerning the body's function as enticement as opposed to the allurement of the personality and way of being. Most young people admit that physical appearance is of crucial importance in a first encounter with others, but state that personality and other inner qualities are in fact the primary measures of value. We may wonder whether these ideas about the importance of personality are not in fact lofty ideals and visions – concerning how young people wish things were – rather than reality-based principles of action in choice of a partner. The notion that beauty is in the eye of the beholder is perhaps not the entire truth.

In contemporary society, physical appearance, the outward presentation, the cosmetic and the sexy have been given an increasingly prominent position, particularly in advertisements, TV, magazines and other visual media. Sociologist Stuart Ewen (1988) considers, for example, that the art of selling oneself is of more importance today. The harsh reality is that the body and its framing are also part of the enormous selection of goods circulating in the capitalistic market economy. A large array of body techniques, dietary advice, exercise facilities and fitness magazines help to reproduce the image of the successful and 'correct' body.

Using their bodies, young people send signals as to how they wish to be perceived and what they wish to represent. In this way, the body functions as an important tool when the young identity is being shaped, negotiated and presented. Decoration and modulation of the body have become an increasingly central part of the personal identity and in the formation of different cultural lifestyles. It is, therefore, hardly surprising that young people in particular, in their various manifestations, elaborate to such a great degree with their bodies, styles, clothes and other important symbolic expressions:

Anna: Just look at the H & M girl, my God she looks good. I mean, it gives you a fucking complex, I'm not just complaining, her body's perfect. She's sitting there bent over and no tummy rolls. (Hammarén and Johansson 2001: 68)

The gap between one's own body and the dream world symbolized by the homogeneous media body can undermine a positive self-image. When adornment becomes a question of personal responsibility, it is the individual who must take the consequences of any failures. Demands and shame may follow. Moreover, for those who are somewhat older, the slow deterioration of the body becomes a challenge that is kindled by the media world's cosmetic mantra and its function as arbiter of taste.

Given this development, it may be surprising to hear that many young people have a relatively positive self-image and are able to put the prevailing fixation with appearances in perspective. When we ask young people whether they think they are good looking, sexy, smart or nice, their answers reveal relatively high levels of self-confidence.

Table 5.3 shows that a majority of both young women and young men feel that they are very or fairly good looking, though young men seem to have a somewhat

Table 5.3   'Do you think you're good looking?'

	Yes, very	Fairly	Not particularly	No, not at all
Men (n=291)	17.9%	54.3%	26.1%	1.7%
Women (n=345)	7.8%	50.1%	38.0%	4.1%

Chi-2: 0.00

greater estimation of their own appearance. Because young women, to a greater extent than young men, are defined in terms of aspects of appearance and are the objects of erotically charged pictures and centrefolds, they have more opportunities to compare their own self-images with the beautiful smiles and bodies found in magazines and on advertisement billboards. At the same time, we see today how the male body is approaching the traditional female body as a centrefold object in our public squares, at bus stops and in magazines and as a consumer group with purchasing power.

In contemporary society, it is increasingly common for men to be objects in the sphere of consumption and for men to be encouraged to modulate their bodies. Consider, for example, the new lifestyle magazines for men such as *Men's Health*. Our data show that 43% of the young men and 63% of the young women agree completely, strongly or to a certain degree with the following statement: *It's okay for young men to wear make-up*. Moreover, 86% of the young men and 94% of the young women agree completely, fairly strongly or to a certain degree with the following statement: *Young men care just as much about their looks as young women do*. As shown in the table, young men also question their own appearance: 28% of them respond with *not particularly/not at all* when asked whether they think they are good looking.

Bound up with self-image is the experience of shame with regard to the physical. As mentioned earlier, young women, to a somewhat greater degree than young men, are ashamed of masturbating, and the physicality of pornography can create ambivalence and doubt among members of both sexes. Other studies have shown that it is not uncommon for young people – particularly young men – to express concern about the appearance, size and functioning of their own genitals, but does this shame prevail generally? Is it the case that young people largely experience shame with regard to nakedness, talking about sex, their own bodies and how they are presented? Or are these feelings of shame only tendencies that do not affect the majority of young people?

Our data support the latter alternative: 73% of the young men and 72% of the young women, for example, respond that they are seldom or never ashamed to talk about sex. Thus, sexuality and the increased talk about sex in society do not seem to constitute a verbal problem for young people. Instead, the sexual seems to exist as an ever-present background noise that is reflexively integrated into the individual and that becomes a part of him or her. It is especially reality TV, talk shows and music videos that are helping to diffuse the sexual and the physical and to make them more everyday.

Table 5.4 once again shows that a majority of young people are seldom or never ashamed of their bodies, and that young women's threshold of shame is lower.

Table 5.4   'Are you generally ashamed of your body?'

	Yes, always	Yes, often	Sometimes	Seldom	Never
Men (n=284)	1.5%	6.3%	16.5%	31.0%	44.7%
Women (n=337)	8.9%	11.9%	28.8%	32.0%	18.4%

Chi-2: 0.00

Comparing Tables 5.3 and 5.4, we do not find any great differences. All in all, we may state that young people are relatively happy with both their bodies and their personalities. We should not forget, however, that youth is characterized by self-centredness and an occupation with personal appearance, which many consider to be a great problem.

Will young people think along different lines in the future? This question is difficult to answer. The naked body has become increasingly integrated into our everyday reality and an increasingly 'natural' feature in, among other things, TV, magazines and films. The ideal body presented in the various media is also the body we are encouraged to acquire. When ideals are pumped out to people, it is also people who, in the end, become their own arbiters of taste. It is in this complex and pressured situation that most young people find themselves. Many are able to talk about sexuality, nakedness and bodies, but when it comes to talking about oneself, things quickly become more complicated.

Concluding Remarks

As we have seen, young people's attitudes are clearly affected by the general discussion on and the political arena of gender equality. Although it is impossible to determine whether attitudes correspond to actual and material changes in the real world, they are at least an indication of movement. When looking at the data, we must take care not to interpret them in too linear a fashion. The trends are complex and multidimensional. In certain areas, young people agree on the importance of treating young men and young women in the same way. The image of subordinated and repressed female sexuality is obviously not up-to-date. This does not mean, however, that young women are free to express their sexuality or that they have the same sexual opportunities as do young men. But the direction is clear.

In today's mass media, the predominance of the gender stereotyped agenda still remains. Pop stars such as Britney Spears and Christina Aguilera are frequently discussed and criticized. They clearly represent an image of young women that, on one level, fits nicely into sexist and male-dominated views on female sexuality. We can, of course, see and analyse these pop star icons as signs of a backlash. But the question is, to what extent do Britney and Christina really serve as role models? And even if they do, isn't the reception of these artists probably quite complex? The criticism of male dominance and the male gaze may easily turn into an agenda in which sensual pleasures and liberal sexuality are regarded as morally doubtful. When approaching these icons, we are clearly touching upon the intersection of a number of contradictory discourses on gender, youth and sexuality.

The changes in young people's sexuality point both forward and backward. Although certain attitudes clearly indicate a more gender-equal way of looking at sexuality, others confirm the more traditional view. This is clear when we consider questions of homosexuality and pornography. As several other studies have shown, young men are more inclined to react negatively to homosexuality than are young women, and young men are also more interested in pornography (Johansson and Lalander 2003). Even though young men are aware of the widespread contempt for pornography, they admit to being aroused by and attracted to sexual images. What may be a bit surprising is that young women are gradually being drawn to pornography. Liberal tendencies in society contribute to the growth of a more permissive attitude towards pornography. Although negative views are still predominant, more and more young people are showing liberal attitudes toward pornography. In the next chapter we will look a bit closer at this phenomenon.

One way is to distinguish between a more liberal level of understanding and approaching sexuality, and another level of understanding dominated by spontaneous and deeply rooted bodily reactions and taboos. When we approach for example homosexuality or pornography, we are also getting closer to the fundamental aspects of hegemonic masculinity (Connell 1995). Although pornography may be interpreted in a feminist way as liberating for women, the more common interpretation supports the notion of male dominance: women are created through male eyes and regarded as subordinate.

In the same way, homosexuality marks out a dual gender order. It is clear that homosexuals still evoke negative feelings and ambivalence, especially among young men. In order to maintain their male heterosexual identity, many young men condemn homosexuals – especially male homosexuality. The lesbian, on the other hand, is often regarded as exciting. Young men are generally aware of this paradox. Young women's attitudes toward homosexuals are more tolerant than are young men's. Young women do not seem to feel the same need to protect their heterosexual identities. As we stressed earlier, homophobia is intertwined with the traditional gender order. Undermining this gender order often benefits young women.

In conclusion, youth research requires a more elaborate and complex picture of young people's construction of their sexual identities. Traditional sexology has neglected the cultural perspective, and youth research has failed to incorporate current theories of gender and sexuality. In this chapter, we have attempted to point in the direction of a more critical and multidimensional approach to considering these matters.

Chapter 6

Hegemonic Masculinity and Pornography

with Nils Hammarén

Today, pornographic material in the form of films, magazines and other products is readily available. The great supply of pornography indicates that the demand for and consumption of such products have increased dramatically. This is certainly a matter of great financial interest. According to Brian McNair (2002), there has been a drastic growth in demand for and consumption of pornography in the USA from 1970 to the early 21st century. The annual turnover of the porn industry in 1972 is estimated to be around $10 million. The corresponding figure for 1996 is $8 trillion. In 1996, 8,000 new porn films were released and distributed to 25,000 video stores across the USA. The Internet has added to the great circulation of and dramatic increase in pornographic material. A large proportion of the time people spend on the Internet is dedicated to the consumption of pornography. One Swedish study shows that almost 60% of men and slightly more than 10% of women spend time looking at pornographic material (Månsson et al 2003). Rather than visiting a video store and risking public humiliation, people can now download films and other material in the privacy of their own homes.

Contemporary young people are well acquainted with pornography (Johansson and Hammarén forthcoming). It is difficult to avoid taking a stand on pornography in one way or another, and the debate and opinions in this area have been heated and are growing.[1] Opinions do shift, and although it is possible to have different views in the discussion on pornography, Swedish society, as well as many other European societies, is marked by generally negative and critical attitudes. At the same time, however, it is clear that, at the political level, attitudes toward those who sell and profit by pornography are not as restrained and negative. In many respects, young people are living in a society where pornography and a commercial market based on sexuality have a strong position. A liberal attitude towards the phenomenon is not uncommon, not least because censorship is thought to be a less attractive alternative to the openness that characterizes a free market.

In a Danish investigation published in the daily newspaper *Berlingske* on 22 August 2005, we find that most Danes between 15 and 65 years of age seldom react

---

1 Lively discussions have been pursued among different feminist 'camps', see, for example Assiter (1989), Williams (1989, 1999), Dworkin (1991, 1997), Strossen (1995), Crosson (1998), Kvarning (1998) and Håkansson (1999).

negatively to pornographic content in advertisements or other public media. On the other hand, many people, particularly mothers, are upset by the fact that children and young people are being exposed to sexual content. Moreover, in many countries today, we find considerable discussion of what is often called the *sexualization* or sometimes *pornification* of the public sphere. This refers to the notion that the advertising world finds its influences in the porn industry and in the depictions of bodies and sexuality that prevail in this commercial sphere. This may involve varyingly subtle influences. Some pictures only evoke weak associations with pornography, while others are more explicit in nature. The question is what attitudes young people have toward this development. How are they affected by advertisements and to what extent do they consume pornographic products? Is the notion that this is principally a male phenomenon accurate? Are all young men positive and uncritical with regard to the world of pornography? Do all young women take exception to it? The objective of the present chapter is to try to answer some of these questions.

Although many young men consume pornography, it is not something they are particularly proud of. Here are two excerpts from a group interview conducted by the authors in the context of a research project.

Does pornography play an important role in people's lives?
Sebastian: No, no, it just makes you horny. It's disgusting.
Andreas: Watching porn films is nothing you're proud of or show off about.

Is pornography good?
Rani: No.
Christina: Some people think it's abominable.
Maria: I don't know.
Christina: There are some who like it, you have to let them watch it [...]
Maria: It wasn't what I thought, that there were only women, so humiliating, but it was more like 'is that what it looks like?' [...] I just thought 'wow, will they get it in', they seemed so big (laughs).

Young men are aware that the consumption of pornographic material is often viewed as dirty and almost disgusting. Moreover, such consumption is condemned in the media and in political discussions. This makes it difficult to deal with and relate to pornography. However, society's strong condemnation of pornography may also make it interesting and attractive. It may become a tool in the struggle against a moralistic and boring adult society or it may acquire other functions. Porn may also be used in a purely ritualistic manner to construct a solid core of male homosociality.

In the world of pornography, women are commonly objectified and thereby deprived of their subjectivity. This is not a question of a romantic and restrained outlook, but of creating a world in which genitals and penetration are the focus. It is by and large the male gaze that defines the scene and the course of events. Many young women look with abhorrence on the outlook on humankind found in pornography, but this is certainly not true of all young women. A growing group of them have positive or at least liberal and permissive attitudes toward pornography

(Berg 1999). If we look at relevant Swedish studies of young people's sexuality, it is clear that sexual patterns and lifestyles develop relatively slowly. Although changes are noticeable, it is also apparent that many patterns are fairly stable. Certain tendencies, however, are clear. Forsberg (2000, 2005) states that, between 1967 and 1996, the number of sexual partners increased greatly for both men and women. Similarly, the age at first intercourse has decreased. According to Forsberg, we can see during this period (around 1970–2000) a change towards increasingly permissive and experimental sexuality (Lewin and Helmius 1983; Helmius 1990; Henriksson and Lundahl 1993; Frisell 1996).

Many of the observable shifts and tendencies toward changing patterns are in one way or another also related to changes in the power balance between men and women. People's behaviour and attitudes have changed concurrently with the placement of gender equality on the societal agenda and the increase in tolerance for different sexual lifestyles. This does not imply, however, that these shifts have dissolved the power relations and injustices that exist between the sexes – only that the balance is always changing. Sexuality and the erotic have often been associated with transgression and freedom, but if we are to understand sexuality, it is just as important to see how it is constantly interwoven with power relations (Bataille 1957/1987; Foucault 1978).

Hegemony and Opposition

Youth is marked in many respects by a search for identity and belonging (Ziehe 1989). Naturally, one important aspect of this searching concerns the body, desire and sexuality. Young people find themselves in a complex field of tension containing different factors of influence. Studies indicate that today's young people show several signs of having more open attitudes toward sexuality than was the case only a decade ago. One-night stands have become more common, young people have more sexual partners then they did before and are younger when they have their first sexual encounter. They are also more tolerant with regard to homo- and bisexuality (Herlitz 2001). Gender differences in sexual behaviour have also decreased, at the same time as there is great variation in types of behaviour. The control once wielded by maritally sanctioned sexuality has been replaced by that of the romantic love complex. Society generally sees being in love and mature and restrictive in one's sexual explorations as virtuous. Thus, there exists in society a relatively explicit ideal that directs how young people – particularly young women – approach their own sexuality. As mentioned earlier, this *love ideology* – that is, the view that love legitimizes sex – has a strong position in young people's sexual lives (Helmius 1990; Frisell 1996; Forsberg 2000).

On the whole, young people say they dislike casual relationships, and for this reason sexual arousal is equated with love – that is, sexual intercourse becomes synonymous with love. Differentiation between the fine, morally uplifting sexual intercourse and the spontaneous, merely satisfying sexual intercourse is still a

Table 6.1   'Have you ever read a porn magazine?'

	No	Yes
Men (n=625)	13.4%	86.6%
Women (n=658)	54.6%	45.4%

(p < 0.000)

strong factor in structuring young people's – primarily young women's – sexual living space. However, this theory of good sexuality is not easily translated into everyday reality. Principles of sexual behaviour and values are often subjected to negotiation and displacement. Both young men and young women have ideals to consider, but, in practice, young men have more degrees of freedom. Young people's morals are characterized by the adult moral code 'everything in moderation' and, in many respects, still by a male-defined sexuality. This is well illustrated by the double standard saying that young women are 'whores' if they have slept with 'too many' men. Thus, we see a fairly polarized picture of the sexual young person – partly with good reason – in which young women stand for a more restrictive, relationship-based and guilt-ridden sexuality, while young men appear as active and sexist traditionalists.

Consequently, young people today find themselves being pulled in different directions between different sexual ideas and conceptions. For young people, everyday reality constitutes a kind of field of tension containing different factions and nuances, where more repressive and restrictive sexual morals represent one extreme pole, and liberal open-mindedness the other. Although change is a keyword when studying young people, we may also establish that many traditional patterns are difficult to change and that young people, to a certain extent, help to reproduce these stubborn cultural patterns. One area in which these more traditional patterns are found is the world of pornography. The typical consumer here is a young or middle-aged man. We also see this pattern in our investigation. But just as interesting as finding these typical overall patterns, is looking more closely at the nuances and shadings in them. In the following section, we use our data to show both the general and the more specific.

Table 6.2   'Have you ever watched a porn film?'

	No	Yes
Junior high		
Men (n=329)	8.5%	91.5%
Women (n=312)	42.6%	57.4%
High school		
Men (n=280)	6.4%	93.6%
Women (n=345)	26.4%	73.6%

Responses presented as a function of school level and sex. (p-value within the category of young men: p < 0.333; p-value within the category of young women: p < 0.000)

Table 6.3 **'Pornography is sexually exciting'**

	Agree completely	Agree strongly	Agree to some degree	Agree a little	Don't agree at all
Men (n=624)	27.4%	23.7%	25.8%	9.6%	13.5%
Women (n=667)	6.3%	7.8%	19.0%	17.5%	49.4%

(p < 0.000)

Tables 6.1, 6.2 and 6.3 present results of questions concerning consumption and experiences of pornographic content. Table 6.1 shows that the great majority of young men, but only slightly less than half of young women, have read a porn magazine (the figures are for people in the age range 15–18 years).

In Table 6.2, we look at the consumption of pornography as a function of school level (junior high versus high school) and sex. Here we see that while young men become acquainted with porn films at an earlier age, young women's consumption increases considerably during high school. Thus, with time, most young people, regardless of sex, have consumed different types of pornography. In our mediaized society, it is difficult to avoid contact with different types of media content. Given that we are surrounded by images and that it is relatively easy to end up on a website containing sexual material, it is almost impossible to avoid seeing pictures of sexualized bodies.

Table 6.3 presents young people's experiences of pornographic content. Do they find it exciting or not? First, we see that there are significant differences between young women and young men. More young men than young women feel they become aroused by looking at these types of pictures. We also see how the population falls into at least three different groups: those who become aroused, those who feel some arousal and those who do not think that pornography is sexually exciting at all.

The French media theorist Jean Baudrillard (1977/1990) has put forward the notion that, in contemporary society, we live in a media-impregnated world, where it is becoming increasingly difficult to differentiate between reality and fantasy. Although this may be seen as a rather drastic view of the media's influence, we may also establish that it is almost impossible to remain outside or free from contact with the pictures produced by and distributed through the various media. Today, there is also an ongoing discussion of the so-called pornification of the media supply. The point here is that we are able to see how the porn industry's aesthetics and ways of presenting men, women and sexuality influence and impregnate, for example advertisements.

While our study shows that certain traditional elements still exist, it also shows strong tendencies towards change. The view that young men's and young women's sexual universes are completely different has lost ground to a view that stresses contradictions, ambivalences and fissures. Young men and young women are approaching one another in many respects, while other areas are still marked by strong tendencies towards maintaining a traditional gender balance. Attitudes

Table 6.4   'What is your attitude toward pornography?'

	Very positive	Positive	Fairly positive	Fairly negative	Very negative
Men (n=622)	19.0%	21.7%	36.7%	16.2%	6.4%
Women (n=656)	2.7%	7.6%	18.1%	37.0%	34.6%

(p < 0.000)

toward pornography and homosexuality remain largely divided along gender lines, but we are also able to observe how young men's and young women's lines of reasoning overlap. Today, young women are more likely to consume pornography and a relatively large proportion of them report becoming sexually aroused by it. However, young women are also the primary critics of pornography, although even the majority of young men feel it is degrading in some respects.

A surprisingly large proportion of young men have positive attitudes towards pornography. But if we look more closely at the distribution of answers, we see that one-quarter of the young men take exception to pornography. Using in-depth studies it would be possible to obtain more information on how individuals who have positive vs. negative attitudes formulate their viewpoints. Some cases might reveal young men's active resistance to the degradation of women, while other cases might involve young men who think it is cool to like pornography. There is no uniform young man here, but instead a scale in which different men manifest and stand for different types of masculinity (Connell 2000).

If we study the first Tables 6.4 and 6.5 below, we can imagine a division into three different positions. Using additional methods, we could probably refine this analysis, bringing out more nuances. But for now, let us view this as the beginning of a more in-depth analysis of the data. The following three groups are found among the young people in our study:

1. *Porn enthusiasts*. This group has positive attitudes toward pornography and does not feel that it is degrading or that it should be censored or forbidden. We assume that more in-depth studies of this relatively large group of young men and relatively small group of young women would reveal nuances and different views on pornography. It is also highly likely that the young women who have positive attitudes toward pornography differ markedly from other young women.
2. *The ambivalents*. A rather large group – more young men than young women – partly agree with the notion that pornography is degrading. This indicates a certain degree of ambivalence. Similarly, a rather large group – again more young men than young women – may be found in the category 'fairly positive toward pornography'.
3. *Porn opponents*. A large proportion of the young women in our study are opposed to pornography, feel it is degrading and believe that these kinds of

Table 6.5   **'Pornography is degrading'**

	Agree completely	Agree fairly well	Agree to some degree	Agree a little	Don't agree at all
Men (n=628)	18.9%	18.1%	28.0%	14.6%	20.4%
Women (n=665)	48.0%	20.6%	20.3%	5.1%	6.0%

(p < 0.000)

pictures and films should be forbidden. Note, in this connection, that 37% of the young men feel that pornography is degrading.

There is every reason to continue and to deepen and nuance the picture of how young people think about and relate to pornography. Underlying the figures presented here is a much more complex situation. We will return to the question of how we should observe and think about today's young masculinity. Is it possible that we too easily dismiss young men as porn consumers and male chauvinists?

Table 6.6 shows that young people generally have basically liberal attitudes toward media content and people's right to consume it. Although attitudes toward pornography are otherwise strikingly variable, there is no appreciable difference between how young men and young women relate to the right to view pornographic material. Even if there may be a significant difference, the percentage differences in the responses are not great. Most young people, regardless of sex, consider that everyone should have the same right to view pornography. Every individual should be able to choose what he or she wishes to see or read. At the same time, however, there are great gender differences in preferences for different types of media content.

In his renowned study *The History of Sexuality* (1978, 1987a, 1987b), Foucault takes his point of departure as the hypothesis that sexual repression increased during the bourgeois epoch. He is not implying that this hypothesis is erroneous, but that it requires considerable modification. Foucault is trying to get behind this repression hypothesis in order to analyse the connections between power, sexuality and gender that create everyday pleasures and that give desire its cultural forms. During modernity, interest in talking about the sexual gradually increased. Thus, this scientific ambition resulted in the creation of new pleasures and intricate interplays

Table 6.6   **'Girls have as much right to watch pornography as boys do'**

	Agree completely	Agree fairly well	Agree to some degree	Agree a little	Don't agree at all
Men (n=635)	89.4%	2.8%	1.6%	1.4%	4.8%
Women (n=674)	90.8%	3.3%	3.1%	1.0%	1.8%

(p < 0.013)

Table 6.7   'Do you become sexually excited when you read erotic stories?'

	Very excited	Rather excited	Not particularly excited	Not at all excited
Men (n=578)	10.4%	36.0%	33.6%	20.0%
Women (n=589)	5.4%	36.0%	35.0%	23.6%

(p < 0.012)

between the body, sexuality and gender. According to Foucault, talking about pleasure outside or beyond power is a hopeless project. Pleasure, desire, power and compulsion are always woven together into something that is later called sexuality.

For this reason, we cannot understand people's reactions to pornographic material outside the context of a specific society, where certain normative views and controls on sexuality prevail. Not even people's most emotional and spontaneous reactions are free from societal influence. It may be difficult to admit that one is sexually aroused by something one also takes exception to. Similarly, acceptance of a certain type of sexual expression may be viewed as manly. Therefore, Tables 6.7, 6.8 and 6.9 may only be used to begin our discussion of how young people react to and deal with pornography on a purely emotional level.

Studies show that young women experience doubt and ambivalence about manifestations of pornography and its effect on their own desires. Sociologist Lena Berg (1999), for instance, sees a certain duplicity in young heterosexual women's attitudes toward pornography: some find it sexually arousing, while others experience a feeling of discomfort. Berg considers that young women have learned to dislike pornography, but despite this find it difficult to check the various effects such content may have on them.

Another discussion that recurs regularly is that of the possible effects of pornography on young people's sexual habits and attitudes. Contemporary discussions often express a concern that pornography functions as a norm-setter, thereby affecting young people's sexual expression. The main concern here is the question of whether men, inspired by pornography, force women to have anal sex. In a recently published study, supported by the Swedish Organization for Sexual Education clinic in Stockholm, of 300 young men (16–25 years of age), those who had engaged in anal sex (57%) were asked to state, among other things, who had taken the initiative to their latest anal sex encounter. The data show that the young men themselves had taken the initiative in 40% of the cases and their partner in 33%

Table 6.8   'Do you become sexually excited when you watch porn films?'

	Very excited	Rather excited	Not particularly excited	Not at all excited
Men (n=609)	36.0%	38.4%	17.4%	8.2%
Women (n=558)	7.9%	24.7%	26.7%	40.7%

(p < 0.000)

Table 6.9 **'Are you ashamed of watching porn films?'**

	Yes, always	Yes, often	Sometimes	Seldom	Never
Men (n=593)	5.4%	6.9%	23.6%	28.0%	36.1%
Women (n=451)	14.6%	13.3%	24.4%	22.2%	25.5%

(p < 0.000)

of the cases. The remaining responses were 'don't know' or 'both took the initiative' (Rogala and Tydén 2001). Studies have shown that consumers of pornography are more likely to have experienced anal and oral sex than are people who have not consumed such material (Rogala and Tydén 1999, Häggström-Nordin 2005).

In the discussion on pornography, one question has been whether it is pornography per se that has given rise to certain sexual practices. Some claim that this is the case, while others see consumption of pornography as part of a broader sexual repertoire that also includes anal and oral sex. In our data, 59% of the young men and 64% of the young women have had oral sex. Fifteen per cent of both young men and young women have had anal sex. Of those who have not had anal sex, 38% of the young men and 8% of the young women could imagine having anal sex. Moreover, 11% of the young men and 2% of the young women have had group sex. Of those who have not had group sex, 54% of the young men and 21% of the young women could imagine having group sex. It is difficult to say whether these different practices have increased among young people during the past few years. With regard to group sex, such behaviour seems instead to have decreased. Anal and oral sex, on the other hand, seem to have increased. However, when comparing our results with those from other studies, we must take into account the different procedures and selection processes used (see Forsberg, 2000, who presents and discusses the outcomes of different investigations).

One common opinion is that it is not pornography per se that causes a given behaviour, but instead that pornography represents habits that already exist, puts its own spin on them and causes them to appear to be commonly occurring. If such is the case, is it possible to say that pornography is the direct cause of certain sexual practices? No, such a claim is difficult to make, however we can see that certain

Table 6.10 **Percentage of young men and young women who have watched (or not watched) a porn film and who have had sexual intercourse**

	Watched porn film	Had sexual intercourse
Men (n=615)	No	14.9%
	Yes	48.8%
Women (n=657)	No	28.9%
	Yes	62.0%

(p-value within the category young men: p < 0.000; p-value within the category young women: p < 0.000)

Table 6.11   Percentage of young men and young women who have watched (or not watched) a porn film and who have had oral sex

	Watched porn film	Had oral sex
Men (n=615)	No	10.6%
	Yes	46.1%
Women (n=654)	No	25.6%
	Yes	60.3%

(p-value within the category young men: $p < 0.000$; p-value within the category young women: $p < 0.000$)

behaviours are more likely to occur among people who have seen a porn film than among people who have not. This is also shown in our data.

We see in Tables 6.10, 6.11 and 6.12 that there are obvious associations between having watched a porn film and having engaged in certain sexual practices. However, we may only speculate as to what has caused one behaviour or the other. The concepts of anal sex and oral sex are, moreover, relatively general, and it is therefore difficult to know how the young people have interpreted them. In this case, we do know how the young people interpreted the word sex or whether they have been active or passive in their performance of these practices.

Our study shows several connections between the consumption of pornography and attitudes and sexual habits. The data also reveal that pornography consumers are more likely to have had sexual intercourse, masturbated, to have experienced same-sex sex, and a one-night stand, than are those who have not watched a porn film. Moreover, those who have watched a porn film are more likely to report being satisfied with their body, thinking they are sexy/good looking, being less ashamed of masturbation, thinking sex without love is okay, and thinking that prostitution/ pornography is okay. There are many relationships here, and the example of sexual intercourse may be more indicative of age than of sexual experience. Thus, claiming that pornography alone influences the entirety of an individual's sexual expression probably constitutes ascribing pornography too much power. It is perhaps more reasonable to claim that pornography is part of a larger sexual space and sexual experimentation that also include anal sex, oral sex and a more fully expressed sexuality.

Table 6.12   Percentage of young men and young women who have watched (or not watched) a porn film and who have had anal sex

	Watched porn film	Had anal sex
Men (n=616)	No	2.1%
	Yes	11.8%
Women (n=655)	No	3.1%
	Yes	13.4%

(p-value within the category young men: $p < 0.043$; p-value within the category young women: $p < 0.000$)

Complex Positions

There is considerable research indicating that the porn industry's principal consumers are men of various ages. Given the immensity of this industry today, it would seem that the use of various kinds of pornographic material is fairly widespread. Moreover, in contemporary society, people have greater opportunities to keep such consumption a secret. Pictures and films are easily accessible, especially via the Internet. Consumption of pornography seems to have increased with changes in the media landscape.

To begin with, we may state that young men clearly have more positive attitudes toward pornography than do young women. This is also in accordance with findings from previous research on young people's attitudes toward and conceptions of sexuality. Many scholars have sought an explanation for young men's consumption of pornography in male rituals, homosociality and in the social construction of hegemonic masculinity. At the same time, however, this solid core of male identity is beginning to crumble, change and take on new forms. Today we see, among men, considerable resistance to various traditional male behaviours and rituals (O'Donnell and Sharpe 2000; Frosh et al 2002; Johansson 2005).

It is surprising, in one respect, that so many of the young men in our study are relatively positive toward pornography, that they feel relatively little shame and that they do not take exception to pornography on the grounds that it is degrading to women. However, this pattern of attitudes should be understood in light of this particular age group's problematic relationship to its masculinity. There is considerable support for the notion that young men are highly homophobic and that they even display a number of sexist attitudes and behaviours. In one Swedish study, Maria Bäckman (2003) shows that young men find it difficult to learn from sexual education. They react negatively when the subject of different sexual lifestyles is brought up. These young men find it difficult to find the words to talk about and approach homosexuality and their own ambivalent masculinity.

In this chapter we have tried to encapsulate this frequently occurring and rather negative picture of young masculinity. Although a large proportion of young men have positive attitudes toward pornography, a considerable number are also actively opposed to it. We feel there is a need for research that looks more closely at the distribution of the young men whom we have called porn enthusiasts and that looks at the variation in viewpoints within this certainly heterogeneous group. Furthermore, it would seem worthwhile to study the large group of young men who oppose pornography. Who are they? How are they different from the group of porn enthusiasts? Finally, there is a group of young men who are ambivalent. They do not seem to have decided what they think. The group of young women who consume pornography and who express positive attitudes toward it also need to be studied. One common conception is that these young women are insecure and are practically forced to watch porn films by their boyfriends. But is this actually the case? Do we see a tendency here toward portraying young women as victims? There are a number of studies showing that young women accept pornography and do not necessarily have negative attitudes toward it.

The phenomenon of pornography has always been controversial. In Sweden, it is often thought to be degrading to women. This negative attitude is also clearly present in the responses to our survey study. As a rule, young women have very negative attitudes towards pornography. On the other hand, there is great variation in how young men relate to the sex industry. Moreover, many young people are ambivalent. They do not really know what they should think. This is not difficult to understand. While many people take exception to pornographic images of sexuality and gender, we also live in a society marked by a liberal ideology. The notion that people should be able to choose to consume pornography if they wish is strong. We see this clearly among the young people in our study. In a society in which different forces and different conceptions of pornography often collide, it is difficult for the individual to form his/her own opinion. Young people must make their own way among porn feminists, liberals, radical feminists, conservatives and a number of other opinion groups.

Chapter 7

Feminism and Reflexive Sexuality

Simone de Beauvoir's book *The Second Sex* (1949/1972) has been very influential in putting certain issues of sexuality and gender on the agenda. It has been reprinted several times and is still considered a topical, classic text. Therefore, it is relevant to begin this chapter by relating to this particular text. De Beauvoir states that a young woman is ashamed of her desire and her own body. Young women are portrayed as passive in relation to the more active, sexually oriented and aggressive young men. Young men are described as being more satisfied with their looks and as being in emotional and physical contact with their desire and sexuality.

> His desire is more aggressive and imperious. Lover or husband, it is for him to lead her to the couch, where she has only to give herself over and do his bidding. Even if she has mentally accepted this domination, she becomes panic-stricken at the moment when she must actually submit to it. (de Beauvoir 1949/1972)

One way of working with this text is to read it as a historical document. There are obvious differences between the situation in France in the 1940s and, for example, young people's sexual lives in contemporary Swedish society. However, traditional gender patterns and inequalities are still being reproduced. Hegemonic masculinity is expressed in multiple ways, even through acts of violence. For instance, recent research has shown that physical abuse and violence toward women are widespread in Swedish society (Lundgren et al 2001).

In this chapter, we will take a closer look at the situation of young women in contemporary Western societies. Most of the empirical examples will be taken from our study on youth culture and sexuality in contemporary Sweden. However, we will discuss this research in relation to examples from studies on the situation of young women in other Western countries. As we have already discussed general patterns, the focus will now be on more spectacular movements in young female culture. At the end of the chapter, we will return to the question of the relation between general and more specific patterns.

> Just wrap your legs around these velvet rims
> And strap your hand across my engines
> We'll run till we drop baby we'll never go back
> I'm just a scared and lonely rider
> But I gotta know how it feels. (Bruce Springsteen, 'Born to Run', 1975)

Angela McRobbie (1989) quotes Springsteen in her critical article on British cultural studies. Young men are the focus of and the protagonists in many classic subculture studies. Youth culture studies on young women's cultural practices developed as a reaction. In some respects, this research did highlight other experiences and activities, but it also contributed to the construction of a number of differences between how young men and young women were portrayed. A clear gender polarization developed within youth research, which contributed to the image of two different cultures. Thus, this branch of research actually contributed to reproducing gender stereotypes.

When we look at research on sexuality and sexual practices, empirical studies tend to confirm this gender-stereotyped picture. Young men are portrayed as active, in control of themselves and dominant, whereas young women are seen as passive, subordinate and controlled by the young men (Lees 1993, Holland et al 1998, Centervall 1995). This dual picture is frequently reported and reproduced, even today.

As already mentioned, this way of approaching gender identities was quite common during the 1980s and even at the beginning of the 1990s. During the late 1990s, however, developments within gender theory and queer theory contributed to a critical discussion of the notion of gender polarization. Scholars developed new ways of looking at sexuality, gender and identity. There were strong influences from post-structuralism, not least from the queen of queer theory, Judith Butler. But this does not mean that the more polarized approach to gender disappeared altogether from youth research.

In this chapter, we discuss recent trends and developments in young women's culture. When looking at research from the 1990s, it is possible to discern a clear shift from discussions on oppression to more optimistic discussions on the active and subversive young woman. In everyday life, the frames of the aesthetic bedroom culture have been abandoned for a public space filled with expectations and desire. Young women play soccer, wrestle and are engaged in martial arts and bodybuilding (Hammarén and Johansson 2002). The traditional boundaries between gender roles are being transformed into a fluid arena of different gender identities. The question is how far into everyday life this kind of transgression and these subversive strategies reach. Do these changes in gender identities affect sexuality and bodily practices?

Young women today tend to use various subversive and active strategies to deal with male dominance. As earlier mentioned, Sue Lees (1993) identified different ways of reacting to male dominance. On the one hand, there is *avoidance* or *resignation*, which are more defensive strategies. On the other hand, there is always the possibility of developing *subversive strategies*. Feminist networks and fanzines with names such as *Patti Smith*, *Diabolic Clits*, *Ben is Dead* and *Pucker Up* indicate the direction for young women (Leonard 1998).

In order to develop a more general picture of recent developments, we will discuss a number of empirical case studies and examples. First, we comment on recent developments in young women's activism and struggle for equality. In the first part of the chapter, we look more closely at the use of fanzines and the phenomenon of Riot Grrls. Thereafter, we use an example of reflexive sexuality

– political lesbianism – to begin our discussion of how certain young people relate to their bodies and their sexuality. Using this as an example of a hyperreflexive way of constructing sexuality and gender identity, we analyse and discuss more common contemporary gender strategies. At the end of the chapter, we return to issues of the resistance and strategies used in everyday life to deal with male dominance.

The Cunt Club and Riot Grrls

The Riot Grrl movement emerged in the 1990s and had its roots in the punk rock movement. One of the central concepts in Riot Grrl is DIY: 'Do It Yourself.' This concept was also central to the punk movement. It involved twisting, turning and reformulating old symbols and creating new subversive symbols. A common device was to conquer a power symbol and then use it for your own purposes.

In his classic work *Subculture. The Meaning of Style* (1979), the British culture theorist Dick Hebdige studies and analyses the punk movement in detail. He shows how a new attitude towards and way of thinking about language, symbols and social reality were created within this youth movement. Signs were detached from their established meanings and treated as free-floating material for interpretation. The arbitrary relation between a sign and its signification were elucidated and highlighted. In this way, opportunities were created to generate new meanings and to use language and symbols creatively. The punk movement was in tune with major tendencies toward change taking place in the culture – in art, aesthetics and the social sciences.

Just as we can understand the punk movement as part of a larger cultural process of transformation, we can also see the feminist Grrl movement of the 1990s as part of a larger change in feminist thought. In the 1990s, the area of gender studies broadened, giving men's studies and queer studies central positions in the field. Although this development began earlier, it was during the 1990s that it was elucidated and new currents of ideas and new theories gained their real right of entry into the field. This was noticeable both within and outside academia.

Riot Grrls is not an organized movement, but should instead be seen as a very heterogeneous collection of cultural and political manifestations. Its more obvious origins may be found in a group of feminist punk rockers and musicians, who also organized parties and concerts, published their own fanzines and made themselves heard in other ways (Ostermark 2003). Although the contours of the phenomenon are relatively blurred, the phrase Riot Grrls still produces a great number of results in an Internet search, which would seem to indicate that it remains today a strong point of reference for young active feminists. Two of the most well-known netzines are *Geek Girl* and *Riotgrrl*. But there are a number of other netzines and chat clubs where young women and perhaps even young men can air their opinions about our male-dominated society.

At the end of the 1990s, the book *Cunt Club* was published in Sweden (Skugge et al 1999; this is our translation of the Swedish title *Fittstim*). It was very influential immediately and is viewed today as a landmark and recurrent point of reference in the young feminist movement. The book contains a collection of texts written by young feminists. Many of the texts concern how young women are subject to violence, sexual repression and sexism. At the same time, however, the book also radiates optimism, resistance and creativity. It constitutes an advanced attempt to reinforce young women's self-confidence and to teach them to fight back against their repressors. We will return to several of the texts in *Cunt Club* in the following sections.

Cunt Club got its name from a statement made by former Swedish Trade Union Confederation president Stig Malm. In May 1992, Swedish media reported that Malm had called the women's association of the Social Democratic party 'a fucking cunt club'. This provides a good example of how young feminists are conquering abusive words and expressions in order to use them on the offensive. But even if the young women who contributed to *Cunt Club* and also many of the fanzines mentioned earlier radiate optimism and resistance, we find descriptions too of how miserable it can be to be young, female and perhaps also lesbian. The following excerpt was taken from Jenny Svenberg's (1999: 107) article in *Cunt Club*.

> I moved from Växjö to Stockholm so I could dare to come out. That was four years ago. I've never understood the gay guys and lesbians who stay in small towns like Växjö and Åmål. If I walked hand in hand with Jenny down main street in Växjö, people's eyes would pop out, then they'd go home and write a letter to the editor of the local paper saying how these women go against the Bible and all that is natural.

There are several similar examples showing how young women engage in active resistance to male repression. The vision expressed by Angela McRobbie in her now classic article is being realized in the Grrl culture (which is perhaps better seen as a collection of several disparate cultures than as a single culture). In the book, *A Girl's Guide to Taking Over the World. Writings from the Girl Zine Revolution* (Green and Taormino 1997), we can read texts from the great number of Grrl fanzines now prevalent on the market. Here are some examples:

By Tammy Rae Carland, from I love Amy Carter
There has been a considerable amount of work done on the representation of female bodies but not nearly enough work done on the self-representation of women's bodies. I've been talking with women about this lately and I've heard all kinds of different stories. One of the ongoing themes of these conversations has been the issue of fear. The vagina is a simultaneous site of lust/desire and fear/disgust. And this dichotomy is internalized as much as it is an external construction. These stories are about women who have never seen their own vagina, who have been afraid to sleep with another woman the first time because they thought they wouldn't know what to do. (Green and Taormino 1997: 67)

Barbies we would like to see, by Lala, from Quarter Inch Squares
Gender Fuck Barbie: he becomes she and she becomes he, and we all end up in a lovely gender limbo. Comes with interchangeable anatomy make-up, facial hair, two complete

mix-and-match, gender-specific wardrobes. Barbie-sized copies of Kate Bornstein's Gender Outlaw and My Generation Workbook optional.

Bisexual Barbie: Comes in a box with Midge, Ken, and a button that says I'M BISEXUAL, I'M NOT ATTRACTED TO YOU.

Single Mom Barbie: One kid to raise. Insufficient child support, a job that doesn't pay enough to make ends meet. Accessories such as good child care, a support network, and a good night's sleep optional. (Green and Taormino 1997: 111)

Patti Smith published writing about sex and death, bulimia, being a teen queer, with a proto-grrl aesthetic. Proto, 'cause when I started it had no idea there were any other girls at my age who identified as feminist the way I did – angry, slutty, rageful girls who took no shit. (Green and Taormino 1997: 3)

Young women with different interests, needs and driving forces are brought together within the framework of these types of imaginary communities. A public is created here that at best serves as support in the complex identity work being done by young women. By identifying themselves with and anchoring themselves to various fanzines, websites and styles of music, young women are able to liberate themselves from the limitations that mark much of the romantic variants of girls' same-sex friend culture. Today, young women are conquering central aspects of public life and colonizing it with their demands for equality and equal terms.

Most interesting in this connection is the views on physicality and sexuality that are created in this media reality. Although, as mentioned earlier, these texts contain a multitude of expressions and opinions, it is often possible to discern some continuity in what is written and said. The fundamental connection here is a critique of male dominance and repression of women as well as the use of imagination and creative language in addressing these issues. We provide a few more examples below:

Three young women write as follows at www.darling.se/nr4/grrls/:

My favorite activity in the March issue is called 'feed the supermodel'. Under a picture of a supermodel is a caption that says something like, 'aren't her breasts rather big considering how thin she is and how skinny her arms are?' And then if you want you can feed the supermodel with vegetables, cheeseburgers, pasta, desserts, etc. When you choose the dish, you see how the model gets plumper right before your eyes, and then you can win a book.

Many of the texts deal with the body or sexuality. These seem to be subjects that affect and engage young women. Many of the fanzine texts also concern self-image, the body and physical appearance. How should one dress, look and behave as a young woman in today's society?

This culture is largely about *empowerment*, that is, about looking ahead and throwing off stale old values. Much of the critique concerns the media. For instance, one common line of criticism is directed towards everything that in any way sustains or is part of repression of the body. We find the following excerpt in an article on role models:

With Riot Grrls, it's the power of talent and attitude. With Ally McBeal, it's the power of the short skirt. There is a major reward that women can look forward to – that we are being recognized and listened to. We just have to make sure that the right women speak for us. As Gloria Steinem has said, 'Feminism is a revolution, not a public relations movement'. (Jillan Freeman 1999 at www.snnrdr.ca/snn/old/feb99/feb99/grrls.html)

Another common understanding in this movement is that there are great differences, but also considerable continuity, between the older feminist generation and the Riot Grrls. The tone among feminists of the 1990s is often described as somewhat tougher, more jocular and ironic.

It is clear that, in all its forms and manifestations, Riot Grrls constitutes an important point of reference for young women. Other like-minded people may be found here, and one can express one's frustrations, anger and disappointment concerning the male-dominated society. As one young woman states: 'After a year's aimless surfing – hearing of American college boys' dicks and 1001 recipes for cupcakes – finally something worth reading' (www.darling.se/nr4/grrls/).

This exposition on Riot Grrls and the widespread fanzine culture has been intended to provide a basic picture of what is happening among young feminists. In the following sections, we will focus on a number of the project's in-depth studies of this group.

Political Lesbianism and Reflexive Sexuality

To what extent is it possible, in today's society, actively to choose how we shape our own sexuality? One common understanding is that human sexuality is genetically determined. But there are also those who claim that biology only establishes certain frameworks, within which we are free to choose our own sexuality. The Swedish psychologist Camilla Kolm's (2003) study of a number of women who choose to become lesbians for political reasons shows how today's young people actively form their own gender identity and sexuality.

Kolm interviewed nine young women between 22 and 28 years of age. These young women feel that, in contemporary society, it is almost impossible to live in an equal heterosexual relationship. The fact that we live in a patriarchal society implies that the woman will *always* be subordinate in this type of intimate relationship. One solution to this problem is actively to choose to give up heterosexual relationships. This means that sexuality is not primarily governed by desire, lust and physicality. Primary here is instead one's political viewpoints. This does not preclude, of course, that such a choice may also involve desire and sensuality. Moa, one of the young women in Kolm's study expressed this as follows: 'I'm not really a lesbian in the first place, I'm first a feminist and consequently it's quite natural to become a lesbian' (Kolm 2003: 213).

Once the political agenda and sexuality have been interwoven, the choice of a partner is not perceived as particularly fabricated. The women's conscious efforts have resulted in something that may be seen as spontaneous and physical sexuality.

This is, naturally, something of a paradox. Is it really possible to think yourself to a new sexuality?

The young women in Kolm's study direct sharp criticism towards our sexist society. They have also actively chosen to have sexual relations with women. This is not to say that they view themselves as lesbians. Instead, they maintain their right to *not* be categorized, labelled or locked into any category at all. This implies that they are essentially open to the idea of perhaps one day living with a man. The point here is that they have succeeded in taking control of and conquering sexuality. These young women do not feel that they are controlled by desire, but instead that they are able to choose where, when and how they experience pleasure with their bodies. They are also highly critical towards societal norms in general and in particular 'the heterosexual matrix'.

At the same time, these young women dissociate themselves from the concept of bisexuality. They feel it is important to choose sides. What is fundamental here is showing solidarity with women and denying all forms of *essentialism*, that is, the notion that there are biological, psychological or other predominating explanations for sexual choice. Thus, this is essentially an identity and resistance project that rejects all forms of classification and stable identities.

These young women take their arguments and analyses from the gender studies literature. They are giving shape to a *hyperreflexive* attitude towards the body, identity and society. Actions and attitudes are constantly being scrutinized in the light of an elaborate conceptual apparatus. Contemporary concepts and theoretical ideas elaborated within gender theory are constantly collected and used.

Political lesbians are different in many crucial respects from other lesbians. This creates a number of tensions and conflicts. There are many who object to the notion that it is possible to choose to become a lesbian. One common description is that the coming-out process entails pain, deceit, repudiation and crises (Lundahl 1998). This type of trauma and pain do not occur in the same way among political lesbians. For this reason, there are many who doubt that it is possible to choose to become homosexual. Yet, people's experiences of this are quite variable. As one of the young women in Kolm's study expressed it: 'I never experienced a really bad coming-out process or stuff like that, it was just completely okay for me from the beginning. I think it's because I made a clear choice, that there wasn't all this shame and guilt and stuff from when I was little' (2003: 234).

Sexuality is often viewed as something that comes from the inside. In contrast to this idea of authenticity and genuineness, political lesbians present a radical constructivism, in which identity and sexuality are constantly being reshaped and changed. This means that they reject the notion that homosexuality has a biological and genetic basis. Thus, instead of stressing that biology is our fate, these young women see sexuality, desire and physicality as something they can shape and influence.

Kolm's study of young women shows how, in contemporary society, questions concerning the body and lust are tied to choice and the active construction of sexuality. Here, we have taken a great step from de Beauvoir's repressed female bodies to today's young, self-confident women.

Everyday Feminism

Resistance to men's repression of women and to the stereotyping of women takes place in many different arenas. The Swedish social psychologists Birgitta Larsson and Anna-Carin Lindh (2003) begin their study of a group of small-town feminists by describing a campaign. The young women had gathered in the town square on International Women's Day. They immediately got to work and started cutting up Barbie and Ken dolls. They even burned a number of pornographic magazines. The campaign received a fair amount of attention, and the local paper published a report including a large photograph of a mutilated Barbie. Their actions provoked mixed reactions. The young women received a great deal of criticism from parents who didn't like seeing their children's toys mutilated and from young men who taunted the young feminists, calling them 'feminist whores'.

As we see in the following excerpt, even the young women's friends and family were affected:

A-C:	Do you think you became famous after the campaign? You said you got so much attention partly because it's a small town …
Frida:	For sure! We were almost like local celebrities. It felt sort of weird at first. They yelled 'feminist' at my dad at his work. He came home and was real mad (laughs). So that it …
A-C:	So you could say your family was held accountable?
Frida:	Yeah. They got to hear about it: 'What is your daughter doing exactly?' (Larsson and Lindh 2003: 154)

The young women found it difficult to gain acceptance for their efforts in the community. This caused them to gradually concentrate more and more on their own projects. They considered a photography project including a series of pictures in which Barbie would kick Ken out of the house only to begin dating Sindy; but the project was never realized. This shows that the community may have a fairly great influence. It is hard to maintain the struggle when everyone is against you and when there is no support. But this is also an illustration of the difficulties inherent in being young and feminist. There is still a risk of being met with negative reactions, particularly if one is perceived as militant.

Although a more constructivist and feminist world-view has gradually won some acceptance, it is far from being conventional and universal. According to these young women, the prevailing picture of gender is still characterized by thoughts on gender roles. It is quite clear that these young women's language usage is close to that found in gender studies. They talk about constructions and, moreover, spend time drawing boundaries between what should or should not and may or may not be viewed as feminism. Although this scientification of everyday life is not as clear as that shown in the study on political lesbians, there are obvious parallels. For instance, consider the following critical discussion of what constitutes feminism:

Klara: I don't think everything the media call feminism is feminism. But … like this Spice Girls-Girl Power syndrome we see now … I don't call that feminism, but it's often presented that way in magazines and all. Being yourself and presenting yourself and you're the best and you can do what you like and look the way you want, but within certain limits. You should be pretty and have big breasts and shaved legs and so on. That's often the image of feminism in today's media and that doesn't fit all feminists. (Larsson and Lindh 2003: 184)

This study of small-town feminists shows clearly how difficult it can be to be young, female and a feminist.

In a similar investigation of young women's identity formation, social anthropologist Fanny Ambjörnsson (2003, 2004) shows how sexually charged expressions and behaviours may be used to put up resistance and to seize a scope of action. Ambjörnsson has studied two different groups of young women at high school. What differentiates these two groups is primarily their class positions, which lead to different strategies for dealing with sexism and men. Whereas middle-class young women largely conform to the socially sanctioned discourse and rhetoric of gender equality, working-class young women show more varied patterns. They are aware of the gender equality discourse and know what they should think about various issues, but they invent their own strategies for dealing with male dominance. This is a question of seizing their freedom of action and acknowledging their sexuality without being viewed as 'sluts'. Sluttishness is transformed into an offensive strategy – into a choice.

Just for a change to treat a guy like that, says Marielle. To see him lying there in bed, languishing, soft, vulnerable, and to just slam the door shut and go. The obvious delight of both the narrator and the listener indicates that this story will turn out well. Although from the outside Marielle's behaviour (dragging a guy from a party, drunk, to his parents' house and having sex with him) may be judged as sluttish, she chooses both to make the story public and to present it as a personal triumph. (Ambjörnsson 2003: 141)

Ambjörnsson succeeds in highlighting the complexity and in showing the creativity that exists among young women. Many of the strategies are intended to disarm and reinterpret male repression. Symbols and codes are torn from their context, decoded and used to create a larger scope of action.

The results and patterns emerging from Swedish research on young women, gender and sexuality are also found, with some variation, in the Anglo-Saxon research. This is clear when we compare the work described above with the articles published in 2004 in the anthology *All About the Girl*, edited by Anita Harris. One could perhaps say that the Anglo-Saxon research on young women reveals a gloomier picture than that shown in some of the Swedish research. For instance, Kathryn Morris-Roberts (2004) writes that, in school-level education, it has proven to be quite difficult to make any allowances and leave room for homosexual men and women or for the bisexual experience. She considers that, on the whole, teaching is marked by an unwillingness to see homosexuality as an important part of young people's sexuality.

Similarly, several of the authors included in the anthology establish that young women still meet with sexism and intolerance. What we are able to state, in light of previous sections in the present book, is that the pattern is quite complex. Today, however, there does exist great scope as well as good conditions for counteracting repression. Moreover, the research has become more hopeful, even if this is not true of the work of all scholars.

Creating Identity

Youth is characterized by dreams, hopes, visions and plans, but also by the everyday, school, routines and disillusionment. It is at the intersection between dreams and social reality that the identity is created. *Perceived opportunities* exist as a driving force and potential. Yet we can also discern *potential disappointments*. It is in this conflictual space that young women live their lives. In this chapter, we have presented research that points toward change, but we have also shown that this aspiration is always in conflict with the demands, norms and values of the surrounding world.

The extended period of youth enables what Erik H. Erikson (1985) calls *role experiments*. During this time of life, it is possible to test different identities and social positions. In Erikson's version of developmental psychology, the purpose of this testing is to move the young person gradually closer to a more stable identity. But today, the aim of such experimentation is no longer the achievement of a stable position, at least not in the same self-evident way. It is more a matter of developing a flexible attitude towards work, family, relationships and lifestyle. The alternative is to decide to fix one's position – to choose a single path into adult life. Yet today this is viewed as an active choice – a decision that must be defended and based on valid arguments.

The case study on young women who actively choose to become lesbians is an example of a radical transformation of views on sexuality, desire and the body. In many ways, these young women are defying common conventions and conceptions. From the perspective of Erikson's developmental psychology, we could see this phenomenon as an expression of the role testing that occurs during the phase Erikson considers to be a type of transition between adolescence and adult life. But this is probably too narrow an interpretation of what these young women are staging.

Several of the women interviewed by Kolm had already passed through the period that Erikson viewed as part of a psychological and social phase of transition and experimentation. Instead of seeing this phenomenon as a sign of pathology or as a sign that these individuals have failed to solve the conflict that would have transported them into adult life, it may be more appropriate to talk about a radical transformation of the sphere of intimacy. In today's society, the realization that it is possible to choose, construct and influence one's own sexuality and body is gaining ground. This does not mean, however, that we are in a situation where everyone chooses freely, that is, free from the influences of social conventions and moral reactions. Accompanying new freedoms and insights is also the creation of new systems of control.

The identity is formed in a *conflictual space* – a *space* in which dreams are set against social reality, opportunities against limitations and stability against change. When we approach this conflictual space, we see how social factors such as class, gender and ethnic affiliation may be transformed into either possibilities or obstacles. At best, the individual will develop strategies that enable the transgression of *potential* social barriers. At the same time, a woman who becomes the director of a company carries with her traces of the conflict that has been established in her inner world. Naturally, this inner conflict may be managed in different ways, for instance through denial, pride or pain.

We have previously discussed Sue Lees's repertoire of different possible attitudes toward power. In the model below, we have used Lees's ideas about resistance to create four strategies that are also in good accordance with the power model presented at the beginning of this book.

- *Hegemonic acceptance*. The knowledge acquired about the nature of society and social obstacles is used to legitimize the life one is already living. 'Often' is reformulated to mean 'always' or perhaps even 'should'. For example, women generally earn less than men do and generally take more responsibility for the children and the household. According to some, this implies that women are probably biologically better equipped to take care of children. Thus, they should stay home and let their husbands pursue their careers and earn the money.
- *Subordination*. There is always a risk that potential barriers will be transformed into actual limits. This may be manifested when, for example, a young person rejects all possibilities of getting a particular dream job or of developing a certain talent. The person perhaps says to him/herself: 'anyway, I don't have the requirements for this'. Such an attitude naturally leads to failure – to a self-fulfilling prophecy. If one expresses something frequently enough, it will become an almost incontestable fact.
- *Negotiation*. Boundaries and obstacles gradually become more obvious. This does not mean that one 'gives up on' one's goals. However, ambitions may be modified and take on new forms. Even if one is highly critical of 'traditional' ways of staging gender, one may easily end up helping to reproduce these patterns. Yet this never occurs in any absolute manner. Many are trying to alter their attitudes and to act in a more gender equal way.
- *Opposition*. Even though society functions in a certain way now, this does not mean it will always do so. Change is often possible and desirable. Reflexive knowledge is often used to analyse and scrutinize society. Strategies of resistance are then elaborated on the basis of this knowledge.

When we look more closely at and compare Scandinavian research with Anglo-Saxon research, we see the recurrence of similar results and pictures of gender. The research largely deals with the notion that power and gender differences still exist. In today's society, being a young woman and a feminist is not completely uncomplicated. At the same time, much of the research points toward change and it shows the enormous potential to be found among young women. The next chapter will focus on young men. Later, we will return to the more general picture, and discuss and analyse in more detail how we, today, may view both continuity and change.

Chapter 8

Young Masculinities in Transition

Self-Assured Masculinity – A Myth?

Just as the woman is viewed as the Other in society – that is, as someone defined in the man's gaze – the man is also transformed into the Other in many texts focused on gender. Which men actually embody the manifest, autocratic and self-assured masculinity we find in, for example Simone de Beauvoir's work, and in a great number of contemporary feminist texts? This view of masculinity serves as a description of abstract male dominance and of structural power relations. Yet when we approach the level of everyday reality, the picture becomes more complex and contradictory.

The discussion on gender and sexuality has largely been pursued within the framework of feminist theory. This is also true of youth research. A lack of nuancing of the young man has helped to strengthen the picture of the one-dimensional man. This picture may have been functional and useful as a tool in criticizing hegemonic masculinity, but the question is whether it did not also help to create a simplified view of gender. Our purpose here is to discuss some of the pictures of masculinity that have been created in the literature. This chapter is explorative in nature; it is part of a search for discrepancies, for what is found outside 'normality'. Here we will deal with alternative pictures of masculinity and discuss the contemporary construction of the masculine. We hope this project will lead to new insights into the issue of stability versus change.

When we talk about *the man as norm*, we are primarily referring to male dominance and to how science, literature and politics, among other things, have taken their point of departure from men's definitions of social reality. *Normative masculinity*, however, refers to something else – to how men have been forced to adapt to, mould themselves after and submit themselves to narrow norms for what a man should be. Here, male repression becomes repression of men.

As we discussed earlier, there exists an established and rather stereotyped picture of young men. This picture of men is recurrent in the media, research and in the everyday conceptual world. It often portrays them as independent, potent and dangerous. But how is it created? What causes many young men to become the bearers of this conceptual world? Is the picture of manifest male sexuality part of how young men think they *should* present themselves? In other words, is this picture normative in nature? If so, to what extent is it possible to get behind the superficial aspects of young men's self-presentations?

In earlier chapters we found that the polarized view of young men's and young women's sexuality was in great need of breaking down (Hammarén and Johansson 2001, 2002). Emerging from our data was an active and self-assured young woman, while young men often felt uncertain and vulnerable. The classical image of the passive woman and the active man was replaced by a more complex picture. This does not imply, of course, that power relations between the sexes have undergone a complete change and that equality now prevails. It is still the case that in many contexts, men occupy superordinate and women subordinate positions. But while it is important that we see and work to counteract repression, it is also of great importance that we acquire an adequate picture of our complex and sometimes paradoxical social reality.

When looking more closely at the everyday and the intersubjective level, we find a considerable number of contradictory patterns. The excerpt below is from a group interview:

Interviewer: Is it important that the man takes the initiative?
Samuel: It should be that way, but sometimes the guy doesn't dare to, then he's ashamed.
Anna: The ninth-graders are gonna have a dance and not one single guy has asked a girl, all the girls had to ask the guys.
Samuel: The guys don't dare to, they're afraid of being turned down.
Anna: Wimps.
Samuel: Their friends tease them about it.
Anna: So what, it's not fatal, if you don't dare to do things nothing will ever happen, it's ridiculous, 'no, OK, no then', then you just walk away.
Samuel: But what if she says no, and her friends come and tease you.
Anna: Oh, my God, whatever. (Hammarén and Johansson 2001: 13)

During the 1990s, a number of studies were published that provided a partly new and more multifaceted picture of young masculinity. This research has contributed to the growth of a more complex view of young men (O'Donnell and Sharpe 2000; Frosh et al 2002). What we see here is a partially new development. Young women are taking the initiative and are no longer merely passive onlookers. Male repression is no longer accepted. In fanzines and other contexts, young feminists make fun of the vulgar man. He is scorned and subjected to brutal and ironic jokes. More and more, young men are beginning to call themselves feminists. Values are changing. Yet alongside this, we find discussions of widespread sexual repression of young women in the schools.

Are young men self-assured, autocratic and secure in their sexuality? There is a great deal left to explore here. The image of the young man has been created on the basis of conceptions of masculinity that often lack ties to social reality. It is instead part of the same ideology that contributes to reproducing the image of the passive and subordinate young woman. In order to find security, the young man seeks out homosocial environments in which he can interact with men and find strength in a male community. In such environments, a macho attitude is sometimes cultivated and, in some cases, sexist jokes are ordinary fare. Yet behind this homosocial surface, we often find a complex masculinity characterized by insecurity and a number of social phobias. How many men do not find it difficult to use a public urinal? Not to mention the countless sexual encounters with women that fail completely, ending in impotence.

In contemporary society, we see an increased *sexualization* of the body. Both men and women are exposed as sex objects. Certain body parts receive more attention than others, particularly breasts, stomachs and bottoms. The demands on these body parts are gradually increasing: They should be perfectly formed, hard and aesthetically pleasing. The gender division based on different traits has been replaced by a classification based on the sexualization of body parts (Johansson 1998). For many young men, this means that new demands are added to their already fragile sexual identities and problem-filled attitudes toward their own sexuality. It is a relatively new development for young men that their stomachs should look like washboards and that they increasingly tend to look judgmentally at each other's bodies. If the worst comes to the worst, this striving for perfection may help to create a new male surface that covers a fragile sexual identity.

Essentially, this development reflects the ambivalence we observe in the formation of gender identities. There is no unequivocal development here. Men continue to develop strategies for protecting themselves and for accepting the challenge of acting like 'real' men. Today, the categories 'masculine' and 'feminine' are being filled with new and contradictory contents.

In today's society, we often hear that men have also become objects – young male bodies are circulating on the meat market. Something has happened, but what? The discussion about the new man made considerable headway during the 1990s. This development was tied both to men's increased frequency of appearance on advertisement billboards and to men's increased interest in fatherhood. The first shouts of joy were soon replaced by more guarded reactions from feminists, politicians and experts on gender equality. The hope of the new man was not realized. How should we interpret this?

The fact that young male bodies are being exposed in the media and advertisements could be viewed as a positive development. It is no longer just the woman who is defined in the man's gaze – this relationship has become more reciprocal. One good example of this is found in the film *The Full Monty* (1997), which is about a group of unemployed men in Northern England. Desperation and apathy are transformed into something hopeful when the men come up with the idea of organizing a striptease show. They have a long way to go, however. The project is complicated by resistance on the part of family and friends and, not least, by the men's own psychological barriers. In order to carry out their plan, the men are forced to meet and confront conceptions of the unmanly and to come to terms with their own prejudices. The entire genre of advertisements, films and other media that thematize and examine 'the manly' and that operate in the borderland of what is seen as the feminine clearly contain a potential for change.

Of course, we may object, arguing that the aesthetization of men's bodies does not automatically lead to a radical change in gender patterns or power. These tendencies are so peripheral that they can hardly affect the gender order. It is also possible to conduct an analysis that instead indicates increased self-repression and the creation of an illusory surface that, rather than resulting in equality, reinforces hegemonic masculinity. The men in *The Full Monty* probably do not continue stripping, but eventually find 'real jobs'.

When we inspect and scrutinize men's bodies and men's sexuality, it is often done via the woman's gaze. Young men are frequently presented as sexually threatening – as potent and turned on. These creatures are ready to pounce upon young girls and take advantage of them. The man's sexuality is 'animal' and his sexual appetite is insatiable. Young men are not interested in understanding their own sexuality, in getting in touch with their emotions or in exploring their gender identity. They are simply there, as pure existence. Just like the young man in the TV commercial who uses his pneumatic drill while a group of women devour his body – a symbol of pure potency!

If we move beyond all these muscles, washboard stomachs and potent male heroes, what do we find? We consider that this field is relatively unexplored. Male sexuality has seldom been studied seriously and, above all, it has not been examined closely. Discussions on how masculinity is constructed often concern behaviour, physicality and the superficial. Young men are observed and studied with a focus on behaviour and action. There is no information, however, on what is happening on the psychological level. In this way too, an imaginary picture of the young man is created. What are often observed are young men's desperate attempts at presenting themselves as successful, potent and capable. But under the surface, we frequently find great uncertainty.

With respect to the formation of masculinity, what is perhaps most interesting and relevant to focus on today is ambivalence, uncertainty, fragility and young men's difficulties in forming a functioning identity. Fear of impotence – which is a horror for many men – is a central aspect of the formation of masculinity. This impotence is not only a matter of the physical ability to satisfy a partner, but has a much wider significance. What we see today is how men look for outlets for different parts of themselves in different places. In love relationships, young men work toward equality, but among male friends they may sometimes act out their extreme sexism. The difficulties inherent in allowing these aspects of masculinity to fuse result in a relatively fragmented identity. It is here, in this fragile identity, we may find the roots of the violence perpetrated by men, of men's problems with being present fathers and of the fact that society has a long way to go before achieving gender and social equality.

This chapter is largely focused on change, because there already exists an abundance of research showing a more traditional masculinity. The material presented here is taken from qualitative studies conducted within or in connection with our research project.

The Tomboy

Girls who act in a way that can be seen as masculine have often been described as tomboys. This concept has been particularly popular in psychologically oriented discussions on adolescence and gender. It has also found a strong foothold in popular psychology and in everyday life. The term is commonly used to signify a deviation or a phase of development. In the field of developmental psychology, scholars have gone so far as to see the tomboy as a stage in a longer developmental phase. This is something that some girls, who perhaps have identified unusually strongly or weakly with their father, go through and are then done with. The question is, however, whether this must or should be viewed as a developmental phase. Other types of analyses of the phenomenon of the tomboy can be made from the perspective of gender theory.

Jesper Andreasson (2005) has studied a Swedish women's soccer team. He has focused primarily on the young women's strategies for creating gender, a process that takes place at a kind of point of intersection between feminine and masculine. This is above all a matter of fending off and dealing with people's attitudes toward women's soccer and of tackling the strong tendencies toward masculinization. Soccer is evidently first of all connected with masculinity. The attitudes and ideas encountered by these young women often concern how people view the combination of soccer, femininity and sexuality. In these connections, the young women are considered and seen as some type of hybrid.

In his study, Andreasson shows how these young soccer-playing women create, through their physical existence, a questioning of the boundaries between the sexes that many are used to drawing. It is in this connection that the notion of tomboy appears, probably because this Gestalt can be used to name a hybrid. Consider the following excerpt:

> Yeah, I am. So I guess you could say I was a tomboy (laughs). Once even, when I was playing, it was the final, the other team's coach came up to me. He said: 'no, is she going into the locker room, I don't believe it's a girl.' He was going to check if I was a girl or a guy. So I have been a tomboy. (Kia, 18 years; taken from Andreasson 2005: 30)

As a rule then, young women who play soccer are associated with masculinity. This is part of the same pattern that causes women who enter traditionally male-dominated domains to be viewed as masculine. At the same time, we currently find ourselves in a process of change in which more and more people are becoming aware that the boundaries between the sexes are socially constructed. Moreover, these boundaries are also becoming increasingly relative in nature. In other words, it is no longer obvious where the boundaries shall, should or can be drawn. This creates a certain margin for negotiation.

But in the end, *the boundary is drawn somewhere.* This becomes clear when we look more closely at the body. To become a good soccer player, you must build up your body and increase your muscle mass. Changes such as these are readily associated with masculinity. In this respect, we also see a delicate balancing act between what is viewed as a reasonable sacrifice and a possible bodily change. Ultimately, the body is the clearest marker of gender. This is also a question of the young women's own subjectivity and gender identity. In many cases, the physical changes required to excel as a player are in opposition to the ideals of beauty and body that characterize contemporary ideal femininity. Thus, it may be ultimately necessary to choose between soccer and 'femininity'. For many young women, these increased demands on them to exercise, compete and reshape the body also result in their quitting sports altogether. As one of the young women in Andreasson's study (2005: 26) expressed it:

> You still think about how it's going to look. You don't just want to have a body for soccer, you want to look good too. That's what I think anyway, I don't know about the others, but it should be both ways. Looks are still important, not just soccer. Like soccer thighs, I wish mine were smaller, and I guess the others on the team do too. But mostly you exercise for soccer, to get bigger [...].

The young women who continue to play soccer and who also are successful gradually move further away from the feminine. Now, their bodies and cultural image are not only associated with masculinity, but also with lesbianism. It seems that the better they become at soccer, the more fit and skilful they become, the more they embody something outside the normative and conventional. Successful female soccer players must, therefore, deal with people's ideas about them as both masculine and lesbian. Consider the following excerpt from Andreasson's study:

> I can tell you it's very common. Yeah, I can. So it's no fun for people who aren't (lesbians). It's not fun to hear it all the time: 'oh, you're homosexual, you play soccer'. You get to explain it, like, 300 times that you're not a lesbian. But it is really, you know, it is common. When we were away with the national team and talked to people from the other soccer clubs, we heard that there's also a lot of it in their clubs. It's almost, not scary, but when you say you're on the national team or play elite level soccer, that's when it comes up. 'Cause in division five or four, there you can be more girls, more girlish. But at the higher levels it easily gets more boyish. Except I don't know really, maybe it's just 'cause the players are better. I don't know, maybe it just happens somehow that it's that way. But it always comes up; those questions always come up. It's almost like you should have the answer printed on your forehead and walk around with it, so everybody would know you're not a lesbian. (Jennie, 18 years; taken from Andreasson 2005: 24)

The example of the soccer-playing young women illustrates part of the dilemma of gender construction. Though we see today a greater tolerance for a more relative gender determination, it is clearly still the case that the boundary obviously must be drawn somewhere. This commonly concerns the body and our understandings of what defines a masculine versus feminine body. In contemporary society, it is completely acceptable for a young woman to have a muscular body, as long as her muscles are not as large as those of a large man. The boundary is absolutely drawn at the female body-builder, who is viewed by many as deviant, as an anomaly (Johansson 1998).

Young soccer-playing women, especially those who are successful, exist in some respects at the point of intersection where issues of gender, sexuality and identity are hottest. They bring to the forefront and clearly highlight the question of *intersectionality*. It is when we take something to its extreme that we can first seriously elucidate the boundaries that exist in the culture. When young women come too close to what is often viewed as the masculine, suspicion is cast on them and they are depicted as cultural hybrids.

In the following sections, we will study and analyse several examples of how young men cope with gender. We will focus on borderlands in which men tend to approach the feminine.

Radical Masculinity

The following section deals with young men who have consciously become involved in the struggle for a gender-equal society. Such young men are often considered feminists. This puts them in an ambivalent position where they must both handle their own participation in male dominance and clearly develop an alternative attitude toward masculinity. This section is based on data from two Swedish studies on young feminist men (Hedenus 2005, Wasshede 2005).

Young men's involvement in these issues is often intimately tied to what is happening within different feminist movements. It is frequently in such movements that men find their influences and models. Many young men also call themselves feminists. This is basically a matter of supporting the ongoing struggle in society for gender equality and equal rights. The young men, however, do not always have an obvious position. They must seek out a possible and comfortable position from which to act. This implies, for example, that they must come to terms with their own background and identity. A great deal of these young men's energy is devoted to self-criticism and attempts at redefining their male identity. This may be manifested in many different ways: everything from feelings of shame for being part of the patriarchy, to involvement in common efforts to combat injustices.

At the beginning of 2000, the anthology *Pikstormerne* was published in Denmark (Sörensen 2000; the title translates as *Prick Raiders*). The authors described their book as a sequel to, among other things, the Swedish and Danish wave of books in which young feminists made themselves heard. The book constitutes an attempt at creating a forum for men to write about alternative pictures of masculinity. Here, a large number of young men write about their anxieties, their causes for rejoicing and their views on gender. In many respects, the purpose of the book is to make feminism a common project, across the gender barriers. An additional goal is to show that even young men can become engaged in these issues and actively pursue the struggle for a new and more gender-equal society. In the introduction, the editor writes that the aim of the book is to create a space for a pluralistic picture of masculinity. The intent is not to turn men into women, but instead to increase and broaden men's scope of action.

The young men who become involved in these issues and who wish to create a better society also encounter a great number of conflicting reactions. They are forced, in particular, to face their own ambivalent images of masculinity. In the Swedish sociologist Anna Hedenus's investigation of young feminist men, we find a clear picture of this ambivalence. Men sometimes feel that the feminist perspective is too imperative and binding. In the end, their own sex is only experienced as a burden. This serves to obstruct rather than facilitate their work. As one young man in Hedenus's study (2005: 70) expressed it: 'I've experienced that I've been like seeing the world through feminist glasses too much. In the end you don't dare do anything, 'cause you realize that everything you do you do as a man, and as a man I do everything wrong. And then you just feel bad.'

Many of these young men have a strong ambition and will to break away from prevailing norms and gender patterns. This is a question of taking an active and conscious position, which can be manifested in different ways: everything from getting involved in different political issues to changing or elaborating one's lifestyle. This is largely a matter of daring to break from predominating ideas about what is manly versus unmanly. There is, of course, a relatively fine line between acceptable male behaviour and fully fledged norm-breaking. Today, there is probably more tolerance of people who break from the predominating gender patterns. At the same time, some types of norm-breaking entail drawing considerable attention to oneself. The Swedish sociologist Cathrin Wasshede's (2005) study of young feminist men provides several examples of how men defy prevailing norms and ideas about gender by dressing or behaving in a certain way. The break itself may sometimes take the form of a manifestation or a happening. Wasshede describes different types of more extreme border-crossing behaviour, such as cross-dressing, where young men buy and wear skirts, just to defy the gender roles.

In her interviews, Wasshede touches explicitly on the ambivalence and uncertainty that marks these young men's ways of relating to their bodies, gender and sexuality. Their uncertainty is basically a question of the discrepancy between their own feelings and experiences and the level of ambition of the feminist project. They want change and to be innovative. But at the same time it is difficult to break from conventions, one's upbringing and other profound gender patterns. This complex of problems extends even to the formation of sexuality. Desire is not innocent, but something that has been and is formed in society. The young men are well aware of this. They have developed, therefore, a reflexive attitude toward desire. What is one allowed to desire? What is acceptable? The following sequence from Wasshede's study provides a good illustration of how this complex of problems can take shape:

CW: Well, then what's the least okay?
IP: Well, you can imagine ... fantasies where there is clear domination and subordination or where the man controls the woman it's like ... if there's a real clear pattern and if there's a lot of it then ... well then it's like it conserves the gender roles pretty much.
CW: Do you think that affects your life then?

IP: Not so much, but I guess it could. And that's probably why it feels like ... like it's really not good. I think people are affected by ... what they think about.

[...]

CW: Are you blaming yourself for it, and if so, how does that feel?

IP: Well. No ... it really doesn't mean so much, from what I can tell. So I guess it doesn't affect me all that much. (Wasshede 2005: 97ff)

We see here a few parallels to the studies of, for example, political lesbians discussed in the previous chapter. This concerns how active political standpoints are transformed into issues that even affect one's lifestyle and sexuality. Here, the political actually becomes something highly personal. In reality, this often means that the young men are forced to engage in self-evaluation and in modification of their identities.

If we stop and compare how these young men approach these issues with how young female feminists relate to the gender struggle, we find certain interesting differences. It is clear, for example, that the young men are forced to deal with their guilty consciences. In some respects, they are as much a part of the problem as they are a part of the solution. This means that they must devote a great deal of time to confessing and doing penance. Thus, the position of the young men is different in this regard from the more offensive position of the young women. It is also clear that these young men are balancing between a more natural masculine, but at the same time problematic position, on the one hand, and the risk of being considered effeminate, on the other.

Heterosexual Love?

In the early research on young masculinity, the construction of the young heterosexual man was seldom questioned or problematized. Instead, researchers have rather naively accepted and based their work on young men's self-presentations. This has helped to create a rather stereotypical picture of young masculinity – a picture also found in mass media depictions of gender. Using the tools provided by gender studies and critical men's studies, however, we can today present a more nuanced picture of young masculinity. In her study of ten young male university students, the Swedish psychologist Lina Paulsson (2005) has captured some of the uncertainty and ambivalence that characterizes contemporary masculinity. The study focuses on heterosexual love and on how gender is constructed in the meeting between a man and a woman.

According to Paulsson, the performance itself and the performative aspects of masculinity constitute an important component of the construction of gender. Thus, this is a matter of 'doing' masculinity. The young men in the study describe themselves as most masculine when they find themselves in situations where they are taking care of, protecting or buying something for a woman. In other words, it is when the young men are leaning on hegemonic masculinity that they experience themselves as most masculine. Consider the following example from Paulsson's study (2005: 43):

Lina: In what kinds of situations did you feel like a man, then?

Joel: For example when you walk through town holding hands or arm in arm or
            something. Or when I'm lying on the couch and she cuddles up to me, it made
            me, or it's like she somehow feels safe with me, and it, I think, really made
            me feel that way. It's ridiculous but it also feels that way sometimes when I
            treat her to things, like. And it felt good when we were out eating or something
            at a restaurant [...] to get to be or to get to pay, like, at times like that. Oh, I
            don't know, it's hard. Then when she stands on her toes to kiss me too, that
            also made me, or I don't know it's also when she wants me to hold her or
            something that also makes a great ... well.

Although, as a rule, the young men aimed at gender equality and wanted to see
themselves as modern men, they often staged situations in which they ended up in
a dominating position in relation to the woman. Paulsson shows clearly how the
heterosexual love relation is created and maintained. This occurs through small
means and often through dramatizations. For instance, couples use clichés and
patterns taken from popular culture to stage their love. Yet Paulsson also shows
how fragile and temporary this construction can be. If the staging and dramatization
themselves fail, the relationship may quickly deteriorate. This occurs in particular
when the young men discover that they are beginning to find themselves in a weak
position.

Rather than viewing the love relation as something complete – as a stable cultural
pattern – Paulsson chooses to study how this relation is constructed, which provides
us with a great deal of information on the processes, super- and subordinations that
are part of the formation of heterosexual love. This perspective also helps us analyse
how young men balance between more fixed pictures of masculinity and their own
ambitions to change or to become something other than, for example their fathers.
Paulsson also shows how important it is for these young men to end up on the correct
side of normative sexuality, that is, to avoid appearing overly passive, feminine or in
any other way unmasculine. The greatest threat is feelings of desire and experiences
that are potentially homosexual. Consider the following interview excerpt:

> No, the idea that I would dare fall in love with a guy is way too charged for me. Or I've
> never like, there's probably some barrier like, deep down that stops it. Plus I don't want
> to, or it would complicate my life even more (laughs) if I was interested in guys I guess,
> or I'm afraid of it. (taken from Paulsson 2005: 56)

In parallel with a liberalization of views on sexuality and greater openness with
respect to different sexual lifestyles, there of course also exists a more conservative
and highly influential view. Just as Foucault has pointed out, boundaries are constantly
being drawn to separate the acceptable from the unacceptable. These boundaries
vary across eras and cultures, but do exist in all societies. Our investigation shows
clearly that in Sweden and probably many other countries greater scope has been
created for reflecting upon and even staging different sexual lifestyles. At the same
time, we must not forget that sexual minorities are often the victims of prejudice and
contempt. Today's young people are performing a delicate balancing act between

wanting to fit into the crowd and daring to acknowledge their own bodies and desires. Certain types of performativity are more accepted than others.

The Swedish sociologist Hanna Bertilsdotter (2003, 2005) has conducted several studies of bisexual men's construction of gender. One common dilemma for them is that other people often want to lock up and define sexuality; a person is either hetero- or homosexual. Bisexuals end up somewhere in the middle. Much of the discussion on bisexuality deals with this indefinability.

In her analyses of ten bisexual men, Bertilsdotter emphasizes the complexity of and great variation in the material. Several of the men have come out as bisexual, while others are waiting and feel no motivation to define themselves as one thing or the other. They are more comfortable with changing environments and positions, which allows them to continue to be part of the heterosexual order. They don't need to question this order, but can instead use their different identities to fit into both homosexual environments and the heteronormative society.

In our modern media society, it has become increasingly easy to find – for example via the Internet – forums for practising different types of sexuality. The young men Bertilsdotter interviewed have pointed out that the Internet has given them the freedom and opportunity to meet like-minded people. They have been able to use chat clubs and other virtual communities to practise part of their sexuality. This has taken place without having to reveal their bisexual tendencies in everyday life. These young men have also discovered rather quickly that bisexuality is not so terribly unusual. Several of the young men have chosen to keep their bisexuality secret, but some have chosen to come out as bisexuals. They have encountered different types of reactions. Some people doubt it is possible to be both homo- and heterosexual, while others think it is exciting and challenging.

Just as political lesbians and feminist men defy conventional conceptions and boundaries, bisexual men are also part of a new questioning of an essential gender identity. These young people have discovered that it is possible to construct and form their sexuality, that is, that there are choices. In many respects, this discovery leads to a questioning of the heteronormative order. But we can also state that it is in no way easy to break away from conventions and deeply rooted ideas. These boundary walkers experience a great deal of negative reactions. As Marjorie Garber (2000: 66) writes in her extensive study of bisexuality: 'The erotic discovery of bisexuality is the fact that it reveals sexuality to be a process of growth, transformation, and surprise, not a stable and knowable state of being.'

Deconstruction

In writing this chapter, the aim has been to examine young men who, in different ways, are breaking from the prevailing picture of masculinity. The idea has been to introduce an element of deconstruction into the discussion on young masculinity. By presenting a number of alternative pictures of masculinity and different ways of looking at the construction of heterosexual masculinity, we have tried to illustrate the potential for change that exists today. Moreover, we believe it is important to provide a more nuanced picture of young men. As previously discussed, a stereotyped conception of young masculinity has long flourished and made its mark on the discussion pursued in the social scientific literature. The same types of stereotypes have also been found in the public discussion.

Coming to the forefront in this chapter is a more fragile, ambivalent, uncertain, unclear and formable masculinity. These young men are reflecting, thinking, contemplating and trying to formulate an adequate male identity. Many things that may seem obvious are represented here as more flexible and dynamic. A number of strategic landmarks in young men's everyday realities together provide a picture of masculinity in transformation.

Another common picture of young masculinity concerns *male bonding*, power struggles, hierarchies and the gang culture. These are part of the sphere of male homosociality. It is precisely this power sphere that is analysed and represented in many descriptions of young men. And this, of course, colours our picture of young masculinity. Thus, talk about young men often concerns repression, power, sexism, homophobia and being alone in the world. Other aspects of homosociality – friendship, intimacy, closeness, community and emotionality – are hardly touched upon. The latter world is left unexplored.

By examining the limits of masculinity, we are able to look more closely at the unexplored world of homosociality. In this chapter, we have learned about men's striving to be equal, their experiences of insufficiency and their general uncertainty as to what masculinity really is or should be.

The boundary between the manly and unmanly is changeable and relatively plastic, but in everyday life it is often drawn in a rather absolute manner. In the study of soccer-playing young women, we see how gender is charged with distinct meanings, how the body constitutes the ultimate marker for what, in the end, is placed in one category or the other. Masculinity is not ultimately tied to a specific body, but is instead a symbolic charge that may be found in different places. The young women on the soccer team are often considered masculine; young anarchistic men in skirts may be seen as effeminate; and young men in general may have doubts about their own identity and masculinity. What then is masculinity?

The question of what is manly versus unmanly is closely related to how hegemonic masculinity is constructed in a society. After having illuminated the issue of ethnicity and how questions of gender also interlock and are charged with ethnic content, we will return, towards the end of the book, to the issues of boundaries and change that have been raised thus far.

Chapter 9

Multiculturalism, Gender and Sexuality

Sexuality and the Other

In late-modern society, social and cultural differences constitute both a basis for discrimination and a celebration of cultural diversity. When we talk about *cultural* differences, we are often referring to differences related to ethnicity or nationality. But cultural differences are equally a matter of class or gender, and it is often difficult to discern a particular difference when factors such as class, gender and ethnicity form complex and interwoven patterns. As mentioned, however, when we talk about the multicultural society, we are usually referring to ethnic differences. Roughly speaking, we can distinguish between two types of discussions on cultural diversity. On the one hand, we have questions concerning the problems of integration and segregation in society. On the other, we find tributes to multiculturalism as a source of change and regeneration.

The media, of course, engage in this discussion in several different ways. Television programmes, films and other forms of media presentation that reinforce existing conventions and misrepresentations of Asians, Blacks and other ethnic groups are continuously reproduced. Although such media presentations of ethnicity are not always as clear as they might be and are sometimes even conveyed quite subtly, they help to strengthen the feelings of alienation many ethnic groups feel – alienation from Western culture and from their own position in this culture. In her books, bell hooks has shown how Western dominance is reflected in various films and representations and how the result of this is the marginalization of, for example, Blacks (hooks 1992). Said (1978/1993) has, in a similar manner, examined the Orientalism that in many ways permeates Western perceptions of Islam, Muslims and 'The Orient'.

However, the media do not only convey openly racist and prejudiced representations of the Other. They also reproduce a subtler exoticism in which otherness is presented as something desirable. Naturally, this exoticism may be expressed in many different ways (Sernhede 1998). In his book on the global music industry, Taylor describes how so-called world music often tends to exploit various types of ethnicity. He writes: 'Authenticity is jettisoned and hybridity is celebrated, but it is always "natives" whose music is called a hybridity' (Taylor 1997: 21). Of course questions of what actually constitutes a culture or of how the celebration of different 'ethnic traits' should be viewed are highly sensitive. Historically, exoticism has had the effect of accentuating certain features at the cost of others; Blacks have been viewed as sensual, sexually overactive and musical, Asians as wise, and so on.

But exoticism such as this naturally leads to the reinforcement of existing super- and subordinations.

Thus, ethnicity becomes exotic and sought after, and can thereby be sold and consumed in the form of images and representations of the unknown. hooks writes: 'Within commodity culture, ethnicity becomes spice, seasoning that can liven up the dull dish that is mainstream white culture' (1992: 21). What would appear to be positive images can, thus, additionally reinforce ethnic stereotypes and add to oppression. hooks writes about overhearing a conversation between a few of her male students: they talked about the great opportunities there were for experiencing ethnic sex, that is, for going in for sexual relations with Black women, Asian women, and so on. Images spread via the media encourage such oral and consumption-oriented approaches to the opposite sex.

There are, of course, also a number of representations that modulate and call into question stereotypes and ethnic biases. However, the risk is that these will drown in the flood of Orientalism and other types of stereotyping that flourish in, for example, action films and thrillers. Thus, in spite of the levels of awareness associated with ethnic discrimination, the media continue to contribute to the solidification of certain attitudes in their audience – an audience that is prepared to consume the Other.

Above all, this example shows how the consuming self can be manifested in concrete, everyday situations. hooks and other authors have shown how the formation of cultural distinctions is drawn into a cycle of consumption. A special way of relating to the self is developed here. Skin colour, personality traits, appearance and other characteristics are charged with cultural meanings, in order to create a desirable object – a body that can be marketed and sold. This helps to change our vision and gaze. This process is deeply rooted in the history of capitalism. Marx, for example, described the objectification of humankind. Our times are also largely marked by people's self-understandings of what, when and how they consume and are consumed.

Whether these processes lead to increased freedom and diversity, on the one hand, or to people being positioned and forced to submit to a certain regime, on the other, can only be analysed in individual cases. In the end, we will perhaps have to choose a perspective that provides an efficient analysis – based on our specific purpose. Some view consumption as a breeding ground for multifaceted lifestyle choices and identity formation. For others it is more a question of discipline and oppression. This figure of thought points out certain fundamental social psychological mechanisms. Yet when we approach concrete cases, we must add more information and use additional analytical tools.

When we talk about the construction of gender and particularly about how young people develop and form their own gender identities, this often occurs in relation to discussions on the boundaries drawn around the sexual (see, for example Andersson 2003; Forsberg 2005; Hammarén 2005). Sexuality and the physical are of central importance to the identity-formation taking place during the teenage years and the subsequent period of youth. When we approach pictures of the Other, this takes on an altogether special significance. Much of what has been viewed as immoral, sexually deviant or perverse has been associated with the Other. This has sometimes concerned ideas about the sexually loose working class, at other times the creation of strong connections between race and sexuality. These types of massive projections have often been about power and about establishing boundaries between 'the pure' and 'the dirty'.

According to Nagel (2003), sexuality and ethnicity are constructed in a similar manner, and often in relation to each other. This is a question of delimiting, categorizing and excluding from 'the normal'. The ethnosexual is often highly charged. Moreover, we see clear tendencies towards building up a moral universe around ethnicity and sexuality. For instance, certain immigrant groups are more frequently associated with 'bad sexuality' than are others. Sexuality is ethnicized.

This ethnicization is manifested in various ways. We have, essentially, many conceptions of how certain groups – on the basis of their customs, manners, norms and values – have developed quite particular and often destructive ways of looking at and relating to gender, family and sexuality. In Sweden, during the 1990s there was a great deal of discussion of honour-related violence, a phenomenon that was often associated with specific immigrant groups. In certain contexts, there has also been more general and sweeping discussion on immigrants' cultures of honour. Another side of this issue concerns the exoticization of the Other. There is no end of fantasy and peculiar ideas flourishing about the ties between skin colour, the body, race and sexuality. It is with reference to these kinds of fantasies that bell hooks uses the expression 'eating the Other'.

The analyses presented in this chapter are primarily based on empirical studies conducted in Gothenburg, a major Swedish city of more than half a million inhabitants. Gothenburg, like so many other big European cities, is marked by segregation and new class patterns. This is mainly a question of how large groups of people with immigrant backgrounds – that is, a heterogeneous collection of people who have either lived in Sweden for longer periods or recently arrived as refugees – have been placed outside society. Cities have become more stratified: Clear patterns are forming in which people without financial resources settle in poor areas and people with some financial capital choose to live in 'wealthier' neighbourhoods. Statistics for Gothenburg show how people with different financial resources are distributed geographically, so that certain areas are marked by high rates of illness, high unemployment and other indicators of inadequate welfare. At the other end of the scale, we see areas that are instead marked by high employment rates and good to high incomes (Sernhede 2002).

The socioeconomic map of the city is also reflected and found in the form of attitudes, conceptions, perceptions and stereotypes. In one respect, people are highly aware of how the city is stratified and divided. But we see great variation in how people link these images and understandings to other phenomena. In this chapter, we will look more closely at and give examples of how place, sexuality and the construction of gender are interconnected. This is chiefly a matter of how young people create and develop their understanding of such things as place, ethnicity and sexuality.

This chapter consists of three sections. We begin with a section on the importance of the social and urban space in the construction of sexuality. This discussion is then followed up in a section on rumours and control. The chapter concludes with a discussion on gender equality and the image of the Other.

Space and Sexuality

The urban space does not only – or even primarily – constitute a physical and concrete entity. It is instead a space populated by and charged with cultural meanings. At the point of intersection between the community's historical background and, in this case, young people's narratives, new meanings are constantly emerging. This local identity is interwoven with certain views on sexuality, which may concern fidelity, purity and good versus bad desires. Young people use the spatial to draw boundaries, but they may also use their local belonging to create tension, attraction or to create respect by evoking a threatening image (Hammarén 2005).

There are many different ways of understanding a city. One frequently occurring frame of interpretation applied to the city is the socioeconomic frame, through which we can readily see how the city is divided into poor versus wealthy areas. Most interview studies show that young people have a relatively well-founded understanding of how the city is stratified and divided (Sernhede 2002). This picture of segregation can lead to various interpretations and be used in different ways. Based on how the individual understands the city and on the picture he/she develops, it is possible to formulate different strategies. These strategies may involve, for example, political work and protest against segregation and xenophobia. But we can also imagine more passive reactions or acceptance of the status quo.

In this chapter, the focus is on how young people use their conceptions of the city to formulate and position their bodies, styles and sexualities. Just as clothes, jewellery or other attributes are important parts of a person's self-presentation, urban affiliation can also be used to mark a position. In this way, an individual's local urban identity is something he/she can play with – something that can be charged and used to reinforce specific impressions. In certain situations, the urban identity becomes an important part of the impression a person wishes to make. By saying or suggesting that you come from a poor area, you can flavour your self-presentation with some danger, scaring others a bit and inspiring respect. On other occasions, however, it may be best to try to downplay your urban affiliation, perhaps instead presenting other parts of your identity.

In his study of a number of young men in a multicultural context in Gothenburg, sociologist Nils Hammarén (2005) shows how local belonging is brought into encounters between youth from different parts of the city. The primary purpose of this self-presentation seems to be to establish a position of respect in relation to other young men. But Hammarén also shows that this is just as much a question of attracting and getting the attention of middle-class young women from wealthier areas. The following excerpt from Hammarén's study illustrates the potential to create an image through neighbourhood affiliation.

Fabian:	Sometimes you wanna play tough. Like maybe when you're at a party.
Toni:	(glad recognition) Yes, exactly, exactly. Then we play it up a bit that we're from Kortedala, then you get more respect than others (Fabian interjects 'yeah, yeah').
Nils:	Really, you do?
Fabian:	Yeah, then you get respect.
Nils:	What do you do? You say you're from Kortedala?
Toni:	Nooo, you just walk around in the Kortedala style. Walk around and like ignore people who are staring at you, 'cause they always stare right away … Wherever you go they're prejudiced like that.
Fabian:	There are certain areas you know …
Nils:	Where do you go to parties?
Toni:	Well actually I've been to a lot of parties at Näset.
Fabian:	Yeah, if you're gonna go to those kinds … there they're known for being rich snobs, then you feel extra cool. You say you're from Bergsjön, Hammarkullen, Hjällbo, Kortedala or Hisingen or someplace, Angered.
Nils:	So you tell them?
Toni:	No, there's always somebody who knows somebody […]
Nils:	So you take advantage of.
Fabian:	Yeah, sure.
Toni:	Yeah …
Nils:	… their fear or … are they a bit afraid?
Fabian:	Yeah, sure they are […] (Hammarén 2005: 190)

In this context, another factor concerns where these young men locate their courting, flirtations and erotic encounters. Several of the participants in Hammarén's study state that it is safest to meet young women in neighbourhoods other than their own. In doing this, they avoid social control, rumours and general talk. This strategy is based on the experience of being observed and constrained in their own neighbourhoods. By locating their love encounters in other areas, they keep themselves free from direct social control. The young interviewees state that this mainly concerns the reputations of young women in their own neighbourhood. At the same time, however, it is not unlikely that the young men too wish to avoid bad reputations. In the local context, there is also a great risk that parents and friends will notice and comment on love encounters. The following is an excerpt from Hammarén's study:

Nils:	When can you meet girls?
Sükur:	When you're in town (laughs). It's dangerous in Biskopsgården (laughs). I mean in the place we're from, the village like, there's a whole lot of talk. So it's no fun to go out with them [the girls]. But really they couldn't do anything, if I went with a girl. The thing is they talk so much you get sick of it, you don't want to hear it.
Nils:	They gossip?
Sükur:	Yeah, they're like that … It doesn't matter to me if they say 'well, he was going out with a girl' like, but it's not good for the girl. They just talk bullshit all the time. So it's gotta be private (laughs) outside Biskop anyway (laughs). (Hammarén 2005: 195ff.)

Just as the city is divided on the basis of socioeconomic factors, there is also a stratification of the city space that may be related to sexuality. Certain places, mostly near the home environment, are viewed as being more charged with morals and control, while other areas constitute free zones. The sexual free zones are often found in the city centre, where young people meet and flirt with one another. This means, however, that these places may become the subject of moral condemnation.

The city centre constitutes a sphere of consumption, where young people meet, eat, hang out and party. Their pictures of the city vary. Some young people are afraid of being subjected to violence – they feel vulnerable. Young women must learn to visit only certain places and at certain times. The city entices, but it also entails risk-taking with respect to both physical and sexual violence.

Ethnologist Åsa Andersson's (2003) investigation shows that many of the places populated by young women are also charged in a rather ambivalent way. The feelings of discomfort associated with a place are also related to sexuality. Young women must deal with a number of often negative representations of their own neighbourhood. They may react by defending their neighbourhood in some respects. For instance, they do not agree with the worst stereotypes about their impoverished 'concrete ghettos'.

This does not mean, however, that they defend without criticism their own neighbourhoods. For example, they take exception to tendencies toward romanticizing and glorifying the ghetto. The young women view with suspicion the kind of neighbourhood nationalism embraced by certain young men. These young men, who often identify themselves with the ghetto and a macho style in an exaggerated manner, are seen as ridiculous. The young women's disgust at this ghetto style also affects other young women – those who interact with the macho gangs and who are, thus, seen as immature and loose.

Place and the spatial are often drawn into the construction of sexuality and gender. To a certain extent, identity is bound to and interconnected with place. These young people sometimes feel that their living environment is part of a stigma and their alienation – something they wish to break loose from. But there are other variations on this theme. As already mentioned, young people may also develop strategies for using the reputation or cultural charge associated with a certain neighbourhood. In doing this, however, they frequently help to further reinforce and market this stereotyped picture.

Rumours and Control

Just as chains of meaning can be created that link a neighbourhood to violence and threatening masculinity, associations between place, reputation, purity and sexuality can also be formed. For example, young people develop and give shape to pictures of how people in certain neighbourhoods engage in more loose and sexually liberated behaviour, while others in other areas are more careful to defend their reputation and maintain a certain level of morals. This division of neighbourhoods into sinful and moral is also firmly connected to the categories 'Swedes' and 'immigrants', respectively.

Another picture emerges here, which is varyingly true, of how social control is stronger in certain areas. In the following example, a medium poor and relatively immigrant-dense neighbourhood is associated with a more restrictive outlook on sexuality. In the excerpt below, taken from Nils Hammarén's study, a sharp contrast is made between two neighbourhoods. This is not only a question of socioeconomic stratification, but also of the associated moral dimension.

Fredrik: Yeah, well, I think so, a bit ... Or anyway how people look at, at girls that they well ... people have higher standards I think ...

Nils: You have higher standards?

Fredrik: Yeah, it's like ... I think if you're a real Swede and live maybe in Askim or somewhere I think ... I don't know, I think they have a little ... or I don't know, but I yeah I still think I've been affected by it. That I don't want to ... well I choose people who are a little more, much less rowdy and ...

Nils: What do you mean by less rowdy? That they don't run around?

Fredrik: Yeah, you could say that.

Nils: What did you say about Askim, you were thinking ...?

Fredrik: Well, there's a lot of, I think at least much more ... I have friends from there, there's a lot ... parties all the time, big parties in houses and all so it's really like everybody's doing all sorts of, that's what I hear anyway, I know those kinds of people too.

Nils: But do you think a neighbourhood like Kortedala, that it's more restrictive when it comes to who you hang around with?

Fredrik: Yes, 'cause I think it's much easier to get a real bad reputation 'cause there's such a mix of immigrants and Swedes. I mean if somebody runs maybe, especially an immigrant, then they have lots of opinions about that and then I think girls automatically, well who live in Kortedala and nearby there, think about it much more than girls from other places. (Hammarén 2005: 193ff.)

The fear of getting a bad reputation has a great affect on how young people plan their excursions in the city space. Precise rules are formulated concerning what is and is not allowed, what you may do and where you may do it. In this connection, place takes on a much wider meaning than the purely material. Certain places are viewed as free spaces, where you can express yourself more freely and not risk being subjected to social control. Other places are experienced as more regulated and controlled. In the end, this is also a question of how different groups will be categorized. 'Swedes' are viewed as looser and more liberal, while 'immigrants' stand for morality and more traditional viewpoints on sexuality and gender.

In this way, the threat of rumours being spread and of negative labelling by those thought to be the moral majority in a neighbourhood may become a dominant factor governing how young people move about in the city space and charge it with meaning. In order to understand how the spreading of rumours contributes to a society of control, it is important to also bring gender issues into our discussion.

The usual picture, supported by a good deal of research, is that young women are more readily subjected to rumour-spreading than are young men (Forsberg 2005). It is primarily young men who control and manipulate young women, using the bad reputation as one of their tools. Another common picture is that such systems of control are more extensive and widely used in neighbourhoods where few Swedes live. This picture is embraced and spread especially by the young people living in these areas.

In Margareta Forsberg's (2005) study of young women in an immigrant neighbourhood, the interviewees reported feeling observed, controlled and confined. They also drew a clear boundary between 'blondes', meaning Swedish young women, and 'brunettes', young women with some type of immigrant background. This distinction pertains to everything from morals, sexuality and opinions to viewpoints on intimate relationships and the family. 'Blondes' are associated with liberal attitudes towards sexuality. Having the position of a 'brunette', however, may be a way of protecting yourself from rumours and maintaining your respectability. But there is no certainty that this will work. Defending yourself can be difficult. The following is an excerpt from Forsberg's study (2005: 197):

Naima: We're used to it. If rumours are spread about us … 'Well, okay …' We don't care.
(everyone speaking at once about rumours)
Maryam: We're sitting in cages! In cages! But still rumours are spread about us. We just sit and …
Naima: Yes, and try to get out.

Can young men also be affected by rumours and get a bad reputation? According to the young women interviewed by Forsberg, they can. However, a bad reputation does not affect young men in the same way or as gravely, though problems may arise when the rumours are met with disapproval by young women. The young women point out, however, that this type of bad reputation may also strengthen a young man's position in relation to other young men. Thus, what may be negative in one respect may instead be valued in a homosocial context. The following excerpt from Forsberg's study (2005: 205) illustrates these mechanisms:

Ellen: Now it's like you see a guy and he's good looking, but you've heard he's been with ten girls … so you forget him. Forget him completely!
Subeila: Really!
Ellen: You don't even want to get to know him. Just 'cause of that …
Margareta: Will he get a bad reputation among the guys too?
Flera: No.
Subeila: It's probably good for him.
Ellen: 'Cause guys are pigs.

In Nils Hammarén's (2003) study of young men living in poor neighbourhoods, another picture emerges. The fact that a young man has had relations with a large number of young women does not necessarily give him a high standing. Others' impressions of him are dependent on how he chooses to present himself. Bragging about sexual conquests may lower people's impressions and lead to social devaluation. Moreover, young men react and act in different ways. For some, sexual experience and macho attitudes are associated with status, but this is far from true for everyone. Some young men condemn and look down on other young men who use and have sex with large numbers of young women. This is a question of morals. Having too much sex is not good. Boundaries around sexuality are continuously being established.

An expression often used in this connection is that the young man is a player. This implies that he cannot be trusted, that he is playing a game and will cheat to gain advantages. Being a player may have positive connotations, but is just as readily seen as something negative. It depends on who is doing the observing and the judging. A player is always straddling the boundary between morality and immorality, between the pure and the dirty. In this way, he constitutes a relatively indeterminable figure.

Moral boundaries are drawn in different ways and with different means. We often find great within-gender differences, sometimes greater than those existing between genders. There is a good deal of research showing how the spreading of rumours and strategies of shame have been and are being used to control women. But this does not mean that young men are completely free from systems of moral control.

There is no doubt that the young women in, for example, Forsberg's study disparage the sexually experienced young man and view him as less attractive. He is burdened with the negative label of player. His friends may view this identity more positively, but this does not apply to all young men, some of whom will ally themselves with young women in condemnation of the player.

Equality and the Other

When we talk about immigrants, poor neighbourhoods or about culture, certain chains of association emerge relatively quickly. Many of the conceptions or discourses formed in society are based on a mixture of facts, fantasies and prejudices. Stereotyped images of 'the immigrant' are relatively easily created and the media contribute to this stereotyping. But it is presumably through the joint action of everyday understandings, deeply rooted conceptions and media images that various stereotypes develop.

If we discuss issues of family, honour, sexuality, culture or traditions on the basis of general terms such as 'Swedes', 'immigrants' or on the basis of more specific categories such as Somalians, Iranians and Finns, we easily end up using excessively sweeping generalizations. We are often eager to explain people's behaviour in terms of their social or psychological background. But, if the worst comes to the worst, this can help to spread gross simplifications.

People create and develop their sexuality and gender in relation to a number of factors, for example, class, gender, ethnicity, living environment, childhood and many others. In some cases, gender affiliation has a crucial influence on people's choices and lifestyle formation. In other cases, class or childhood is the deciding factor. It is most often a matter of complex interactions between different factors. This does not imply, however, that we create ourselves in a social and cultural vacuum. On the contrary, it is through culture and the social that our identities are charged in various ways.

What significance, then, does ethnic background have for the formation of different views on sexuality and gender equality? Here, it is important that we take exception to stereotypes, which in an unsophisticated manner connect tradition to identity to ethnic affiliation to sexuality. If we talk about honour-related violence or patriarchal values while tying these phenomena to the category 'immigrant', we are, naturally, helping to create such stereotypes.

In this chapter, we have tried to show how young people living in multicultural neighbourhoods use various stereotypes to construct and develop their identities. The attitudes vary. While the ghetto style can be used to command respect, thereby becoming a form of resistance to the legitimate culture, such behaviour can also lead to the reinforcement of stereotyped pictures of an immigrant neighbourhood.

The young people who have participated in various Swedish studies of youth in multicultural neighbourhoods show great variation in their attitudes, values and thoughts on issues of gender, sexuality and equality (Andersson 2003; Forsberg 2005; Hammarén 2005). It is not in any way possible to unequivocally link ethnic background to a specific attitude. This does not mean, of course, that there are no connections between traditional values, social background and ethnic affiliation, just that it is difficult to map and analyse these connections without lapsing into stereotypes and gross simplifications.

In her dissertation entitled *Inte samma lika – identifikationer hos tonårsflickor i en multietnisk stadsdel* (*Not the Same Alike – Identifications of Teenage Girls in a Multiethnic Neighborhood*, 2003), Åsa Andersson interviews teenage girls living in a multiethnic neighbourhood in Gothenburg. Here, Andersson presents the limits as well as possibilities of the girls' identity formation. The interviews reveal many examples of reinterpretation of origins, strategies for handling prejudice and complex attitudes toward 'the Swedish' and 'the foreign'. The following is an excerpt from an observation of how one group of girls organized an event they called The Miss World Show. The girls got their inspiration from beauty pageants, but reshaped things to create their own adaptation. The idea was to invite family and friends to a party and to present the various national costumes. The different Misses were announced and then came up onto the stage: 'One of them was "Miss Assyria". Up onto the stage wearing an Assyrian costume, and accompanied by Assyrian music, walked Nadia. The girls had decided together to let Assyria, a country the Assyrian girls themselves largely associated with orthodox Christianity, be represented by a Muslim Somalian girl' (Andersson 2003: 171).

Andersson considers that, by making their own adaptation and changing the concept, the girls succeeded in staging a subtle yet powerful anti-racism campaign. The example shows how music, dance, clothes and other means of cultural expression may be used to create a space for reflection and serve as the basis for criticism of and resistance to the prejudiced actions and attitudes of the parent generation. The example also shows how young people are able to relate to social and cultural conditions and circumstances in a constructive and active way. Thus, the examples above reveal how collective structures, and thereby a potential for change, may be created. By using symbolic means of expression and popular culture, young people can make their own contribution to the discussion on multiethnic neighbourhoods and the growing alienation in Swedish society.

The purpose of this chapter has not been to establish connections, but instead to show how young people develop their identities in a cultural field of tension in which various conceptions and fantasies are used to construct the identity. The effects of rumours and strategies of shame are very real and sometimes dreadful. But here, our primary aim has been to show how strong discursive conceptions of differences can result in the establishment of moral and aesthetic boundaries.

PART IV
Conclusions and Epilogue

Chapter 10

Youth in a Post-Traditional Society

> The increasing scope for personal expectations, dreams and longings and the limited opportunities to put these into action add to our internal conflicts. The less traditions spare us (but thereby also take from us) from responsibility, perspective and decisions, the more urgent become our own decision conflicts and awareness of our own inadequacy. (Ziehe, 1989: 156)

People's dreams, longings, desires and search for identity have fascinated and been the object of study of authors, artists, film directors, scholars and others interested in the human project. There is, however, variation in how identity has been viewed and conceptualized. Some believe that the human identity or nature is fixed and unchanging, while others consider that we have a plastic and, thus, highly changeable identity. These positions constitute two extremes in the discussion on identity formation, but in between them we find a number of theories on and conceptualizations of identity. Is there an authentic identity at all? Is it just a question of clearing away everything that distracts and distorts and then presenting what is unique and true? Or is the identity instead a social construction, that is, the result of societal and cultural influence? These questions are of great relevance to this book.

When we look more closely at the empirical data presented here, we see clearly how young people today actively relate to creating and constructing their own sexuality. They are often aware that there are moral and normative limits to what can be done and what is possible. But at the same time, we find a number of examples of how young people try to transgress and defy these boundaries. Thus, while young people are aware that limits are set and that factors such as gender, ethnicity and class play a role in and affect people's freedom, they also cultivate a basically liberal idea about individual choice and freedom to choose one's own sexuality and way of staging gender.

The idea behind this final chapter is to bring the book full circle and to comment on the rich variety of material presented here. One of my ambitions has been to present a good deal of data and material from Swedish research projects and to place this material in a larger academic context. For this reason, I have discussed my own and my colleagues' research primarily in light of the Anglo-Saxon discussion on gender and sexuality. The purpose here has not been to compare different results systematically or to study cultural differences. What we see is that there are more similarities than differences. But to study this seriously, we must design research projects aimed at such questions. What we can see is how the theoretical discussion on gender and sexuality has tended to change from the 1970s to the present and how both Swedish and Anglo-Saxon research follows these shifts in perspective. Whereas the focus in the 1970s and 1980s was on differences, it is more popular today to talk about change, transgression and similarities. My ambition has been to start from discussions originating in gender studies and study both how hegemonic structures tend to help reproduce differences – though not always – and how people then relate, in different ways, to reproductions of these differences. By using different kinds of empirical data and by providing a good overview of the discussions pursued and the research conducted, I hope to help produce a complex and adequate picture of young people's construction of sexuality and gender.

The TV programme *Extreme Makeover* was shown on the Swedish channel TV5 in the autumn of 2004. Viewers followed a number of people of different ages who had been given the opportunity to undergo plastic surgery as well as a time-consuming beauty programme. The main focus was on the operations, but participants were also offered an extensive exercise and diet programme as well as sessions with a stylist and a hairdresser. At the end of the programme, viewers watched while the participants were reunited with their relatives after seven weeks on the programme. The surprised and happy faces of the relatives were presented along with before and after pictures, allowing us to see what had happened to participants' appearances in seven weeks. Most participants were women. We met, for example, a young woman who was not satisfied with her weight. She wanted liposuction, breast surgery to make her breasts larger and firmer and to remove fat around her chin. That same autumn an English documentary was also shown on TV4 called *Cosmetic Kids*. Some of the children and young people who participated had suffered for years with, for example, protruding ears or obesity. But viewers also met a young woman who wanted firmer and larger breasts. Today, more and more young people are turning to plastic surgeons. Cosmetic surgery has become normalized. TV programmes such as these also serve as advertisements.

In discussions on identity and society, liberal ideas about individual freedom and opportunity are placed in sharp contrast to a sociological problematization of biological or social obstacles. The point of departure for this book is that people are born into a certain class, a certain body and a certain national affiliation and that this will largely characterize and frame their identity formation. This is not to say, however, that it isn't possible to change class or alternate gender identity. At the point of intersection that arises between the subjective – our hopes, choices, opportunities, visions and dreams – and the objective – our social and material obstacles – we find a space for the creation of lifestyles and various identity projects.

Sexuality, Gender and Identity

The notion that adults and young people have become more sexually liberated requires some modification. As shown by English sociologist Anthony Giddens (1992), our potential to choose partners, get divorced, experiment with sex and acknowledge our sexuality and pleasures has increased. But this does not mean that all of the limitations, norms and moral taboos that regulate sexuality have ceased to exist. Yet it is important to study shifts in these things, small or great changes, modifications and the emergence of new forms of pleasure. Scientific investigations show that young people find it difficult to talk about masturbation and to admit that they engage in it; menstruation can cause young women to feel disgust and young men often have complexes about how their penis looks. It is also not uncommon for young men to take exception to and show contempt for homosexuals (Martin 1996; Steinberg et al 1997). This would seem to indicate that young people's social and sexual reality is still largely characterized by varyingly limited norms and ways of viewing sexuality.

The romantic love complex Giddens writes about still has a hegemonic position in young people's lives. This can be briefly summarized as the idea that love and sexuality belong together and that sex without love is problematic. This constantly recurring differentiation between sex – as something more spontaneous and emotionless – and love – as something fine and noble – structures young people's sexual universe. This is not to say that the distinction functions in practice, but rather that it makes acceptance of sexuality and desire problematic. There is always a danger that sex will be judged as dirty, less worthy, reprehensible and simply bad, while love is viewed as pure and good (Douglas 1966).

Young people create their own models of how they will view and relate to questions concerning sexuality and cohabitation. This occurs, however, within established frameworks and with regard to the predominating norms and regulations for sexuality in the culture. Naturally, one's own socialization in the group and among friends is partially different from that which society promotes through the schools and information, but still we find among young people views ranging from the most conservative to the most liberal (Helmius 1990). Thus, when we talk about young people, we are seldom dealing with a homogeneous category, but instead with different groups and formations.

It is difficult to study how young people view and act out their sexuality because, among other reasons, this area is imbued with a number of ways of looking at sexuality and gender – ways that are often contradictory. The ideal of fidelity is mixed with a positive outlook on unrestrained sexuality; openness towards, for example homosexuality is combined with contempt and homophobia; openness and shamelessness are replaced by shame and guilt in the face of sexuality, and so on.

Have things changed? It is difficult to answer this question. If we look at results from two of the more extensive studies of young people and sexuality conducted in Sweden during the 1980s and 1990s – by Lewin and Helmius (1983; the title translates as *Youth and Sexuality*) and Henriksson and Lundahl (1993; the title translates as *Youth, Sexuality, Gender Roles*) – we see, among other things, that the ideal of fidelity shows a high degree of continuity over time. But is it also becoming increasingly problematic to uphold and defend this ideal? The latter study, to a greater extent than the former, discusses homosexual young people's difficulties with coming out as well as the frequency of anal sex. This investigation does not indicate that, for example anal sex is particularly frequently occurring among young people. These two studies are difficult to compare, however, as they are based on partially different questions and theoretical interests, yet they do show a high degree of continuity in terms of young people's sexual experiences.

Today, young people find themselves in a field of tension between stricter sexual morals and sexual liberation, between gender repression and sexual equality, between giving shape to new types of sexual patterns and falling into traditional social forms. In this respect, the role of the media may be both to conserve and to liberate. Certain TV programmes advocate and help to reconstruct the middle-class romantic love complex, while others discuss, for example sex between friends or bi-/homosexuality more openly. What we do see are a number of questions that it has not previously been possible to discuss.

When we talk about sexuality or about how young people construct their gender identities, we are also discussing questions concerning development, adolescence and identity. In the following sections, I will position our discussion of sexuality in a somewhat larger context and look more closely at how different approaches affect our understanding of young people's lives.

Developmental Psychology and Modern Youth

There are many ways to approach the period of youth theoretically. In developmental psychology, the tendency has been to segment and conceptualize this period of life, from early puberty to late youth, in terms of different developmental phases. In psychological research, the idea of developmental phases is crucial to understanding teenagers. Here, psychologists conceive of a kind of maturation process, whereby emotions and cognitive abilities gradually develop, are refined and take on more mature forms. Sociological research, in contrast, has focused on the societal patterns enveloping the period of youth. This may concern consumption, views on work, the family or other social patterns. Thus, research efforts in developmental psychology and sociology focus on partially different processes and phenomena. At the same time, it is almost impossible to study young people without trying to form opinions about the relation between the internal and external world. The question is how we can bring together knowledge from developmental psychology and social scientific theories.

Authors such as Erik H. Erikson, Peter Blos and James Marcia have contributed in different ways to the development of theories concerning the internal reality of adolescence. I will not discuss these theories in detail, but instead comment on the developmental psychology paradigm. For this reason, I will shed light on certain general characteristics of these theories.

- *The developmental line of thought.* Although developmental psychology theoreticians do stress that development occurs in interplay with the surrounding world, attention is directed almost entirely towards internal processes and what is called psychological maturity. When society is included in the analyses, the picture of its impact on socialization is often quite static. The prevailing idea is that development occurs in steps and that the individual gradually becomes more competent and mature. In order to reach a stage of maturity, one must be able to cope with a number of developmental challenges. Blos, for example, emphasizes the importance of individuals going through a second individuation from their parents, thereby freeing themselves on the internal psychological plane. Erikson talks about identity confusion and role confusion. This is about experimenting with various roles in order to find one's own identity. Marcia, who has worked to further develop Erikson's theory, talks about achieved identity. However, as we have seen in this book, experiments and the will to transcend prevailing boundaries do not necessarily belong to a specific developmental phase, but may constitute part of a lifestyle. Thus, the boundary between adolescence and adulthood has become vaguer.

- *The normative dimension.* Theories of developmental psychology contain definite statements concerning what maturity is, how sexuality is formed and what constitutes 'good development'. What is often missing is a more detailed discussion on the nature of the relation between the individual and society. For instance, Blos's theory is based on the assumption that normal sexual development results in heterosexual love. However, this outlook is not unproblematic in today's society (Butler 1990). Psychoanalytic theory construction has had great problems with updating and adapting its outlook on sexuality and gender to contemporary discussions on gender, the family and equality. Marcia, in contrast to Erikson, believes that normal development results in the individual becoming what he calls an achiever. This refers to a young person who satisfies societal requirements for entering adult life: work, relationships, family and a social life. Here, individuals who continue to experiment with roles and identities and who do not achieve a stable identity are viewed as abnormal. What is generally sought is stability and adaptation to prevailing societal morals and regulations.

- *The universal identity.* The developmental line of thought described by these theoreticians is considered to apply to all young people, regardless of class, gender, ethnicity and other social affiliations. Thus, this is a question of general and universal theories concerning how human beings develop. This implies that deviations from general paths of development are viewed as pathologies or signs of inadequate development. Recently, scholars in gender and cultural studies, among others, have directed strong criticism at this type of universalistic thinking.

It is interesting to note that the developmental psychology literature and research focused on adolescence has not changed a great deal since the 1960s and 1970s, particularly with regard to theory development. Textbooks and research are still based on the above-mentioned theories. At most, we see adjustments in certain lines of reasoning and small changes in the conceptual apparatus (Kroger 1989). Many concepts – for example instincts, the unconscious, psychosexual development, the

Oedipus complex, psychosocial moratorium and achievers – are equally useful and self-evident today. Thus, this area largely lacks a modern conceptual apparatus. The question is also to what degree the developmental line of thought is fruitful, particularly when analysing the period of youth. It is difficult, for example, to imagine a definite pattern of sexual development that moves people closer to some form of maturity. What happens, then, with people who decide to come out as adults or who choose a bisexual lifestyle? The point here is that it is difficult to identify simple phases in any hypothetical development – sexuality is more complicated than that.

As we move from psychological theories towards the sociological concept of youth, things become more complex. The first thing we think about is the teenage years or early puberty. At the same time, the boundary between young and adult has become increasingly plastic and flexible. When does one become an adult? There is, naturally, a great deal of variation here. Most people, however, do acknowledge at a certain point that they have entered into adulthood. This may be a matter of having acquired a house, a car and children, or of realizing that one's body has started ageing. The definition of adulthood is highly subjective and individual. Moreover, the whole picture is additionally complicated by the pursuit of youthfulness that characterizes our contemporary media and consumption culture. The concept of youthfulness includes a number of goals, for example people's longing for a young and beautiful body and their will to maintain a more youthful lifestyle. But adult life does not necessarily imply choosing to give shape to a specific type of sexuality. It is not necessary to conceive of experimentation and alternative lifestyles as a developmental phase belonging to the teenage years. The tendencies and changes we see in the data presented here seem to show that we must do some rethinking regarding the relation between development, maturity and sexuality. Thus, this chapter moves in a sphere between theories of adolescence versus those of youth as a social and cultural phenomenon, between psychology and sociology – thus in a field often called social psychology.

Identity and Society

Contemporary society is often described in terms of its increased complexity. Traditions, norms and values have gradually dissolved, which means that individuals today must find their own paths in life to a greater extent. Some authors talk about a modern boundlessness. Social theoreticians also talk about a post-traditional society. But what is it that characterizes the modern identity? Since the 1970s, theoreticians have developed concepts to help them analyse and capture the processual and multifaceted nature of the human identity. The following concepts may be used to analyse the post-traditional identity:[1]

---

1 These concepts have been borrowed from Peter Berger et al (1974), but I have reworked and developed them as well as being influenced by more recent discussions of

- *Relative openness.* Identity is not defined unequivocally on the basis of familial ties, parents' class affiliation, ethnic affiliation or gender. The individual must become involved in this project and develop his/her own identity. This implies that the scope of identity work is relatively large. The post-traditional identity is marked by a break from ideas of continuity and historical stability. There are no given traditions that control and regulate people's lives. It is instead the case that what we sometimes see as traditions are questioned, reconstructed and staged in constantly new ways. The identity is marked by openness, complexity and recurrent questioning of what is given to be self-evident or 'natural'. This becomes clear when we consider the issues discussed in this book. Today's young people do not have the same respect for biologically determined sex or for sexuality as a force of nature, but instead tend to view sexuality and gender as modifiable – as things that can be changed in different directions. We can then see how this is manifested differently, from those who see sexuality as completely constructed to those who believe in the role of biology in shaping sexuality and gender.
- *Differentiation.* Individuals move between different social environments and make use of a number of different identifications in creating their own identity. This helps to create a stable, but also complex and multifaceted identity. For instance, at the beginning of the 20th century in many parts of the world, the masculine identity was connected with work, while women formulated their identity in relation to the home and children. These circumstances are changing now, which results in more complex identifications. Thus, it is no longer self-evident that men identify themselves with their fathers and women with their mothers. Swedish psychologist Margot Bengtsson (2001) has shown that it is quite common for young men to identify themselves with their mothers, particularly when the mother's education level is higher than the father's.
- *Reflexivity.* Today, people are more or less forced to consider and use in their everyday lives the enormous flood of new knowledge, perspectives and attitudes that wash over them. Regardless of the subject matter – raising children, health, retirement or relationships – people have access to no end of advice, suggestions and bits of knowledge concerning how they should deal with various problems or situations. However, those who choose to distance themselves from this information, and resist the influence of the information society, find themselves outside the reflexive society. They are forced constantly to fend off new information and formulate their resistance in relation to existing knowledge.
- *Individuation.* The individual project is put in focus, which results in a strong charging of and focus on the ego. This, in turn, leads to a new way of relating to and viewing collective affiliation. The individual then asks: 'What's in it for me?' This creates a reflexive attitude toward the collective. However, it does

---

modernity presented by, among others, Zygmunt Bauman (1990), Anthony Giddens (1991) and Thomas Ziehe (1989).

not mean that people will reject collective forms of community. It also does not mean the end of the social, but instead a new orientation and alternative ways of shaping collective communities.

English sociologist Anthony Giddens considers that we can talk about a reflexive identity project. Today, people write their own stories and actively construct their sexuality (Plummer 1995, 1996). There is also an accentuated tendency toward questioning social and material boundaries. The notion that it is possible to choose one's sexuality, body, profession, life and ways of relating to social reality is strong. At the same time, we know that, in many cases, there is a huge gap between expectations and actual opportunities.

Modern information technologies such as the Internet, mobile phones and other interactive media enable a completely new kind of communication. Today, it is possible to become a member of a collective community that only exists on the Internet. Such a community is different in several ways from previous types of collectives. Although one is never physically integrated with other members, there still emerges some form of shared community. These types of imaginary alliances may be of great importance in young people's identity work (Johansson 2002). Hanna Bertilsdotter's (2003) study of young bisexual men revealed that the Internet and various sites for bisexuals were of great importance to how these young men viewed and constructed their identity. Via the Internet, the young men came into contact with other bisexual young people and discovered that it is possible to develop a bisexual identity.

Another contemporary tendency concerns new attitudes toward time and permanency. Today, everyday life is marked by dissolution and a feeling of absence of permanency. It is no longer possible to assume that a family will stay together forever or that the job you have will be for life. The notion of a stable and permanent identity has been partially called into question. Instead we imagine there are opportunities for change, breaking up and new orientation. Individuals choose the collectives they wish to belong to as well as how long they wish to belong. Naturally, this freedom to choose affects young people's ideas about fidelity and the permanency of relationships. What we see from this study is that young people have developed a pragmatic attitude towards romance and fidelity. Romantic thinking still constitutes a foundation in young people's lives, but they are willing to modify their views on fidelity, relationships and permanency.

People today are confronted with a number of often-difficult choice situations. We are in many ways doomed to reflect and choose. This can be perceived as positive and stimulating, but also as a constraint and a nuisance. Polish sociologist Zygmunt Bauman (1990) considers that people try to avoid such situations by reducing their choices, creating clear-cut categories and finding quick solutions to various problems. But efforts to avoid insecurity are often doomed to failure. According to Bauman, modern society is characterized by ambivalence and insecurity. If the worst comes to the worst, an exaggerated search for order and rationality can lead to more insecurity and chaos. At the same time, most people need structure and cognitive tools in order to orient themselves in life.

Reflexive attitudes towards the body and identity often imply that social and psychological boundaries are being challenged and questioned. This, of course, creates new insecurities and questions. It is certainly possible to change one's body drastically and to carve out forms that are considered attractive, but there are limits here too – particularly limits set by the reactions of others. How far can makeovers go in today's society and still be acceptable? What is clear is that the boundary for acceptability is shifting and changing. As previously mentioned, we can now talk about a normalization of cosmetic surgery. Similarly, we can see how views on sexuality are changing drastically. Acceptance of non-heterosexual relationships has increased, but despite this we still see a great deal of intolerance and violence toward homosexuals. When the boundaries of what is viewed as normal versus abnormal shift, many people feel provoked and want to restore order. The identity is always created in a social and cultural context. Thus, when we talk about choices, reflexivity, flexibility and transformations of identity, it is important to ground our discussion in a larger societal context.

Possibilities and Limitations

Young people's lives and identities are formed at the point of intersection between dreams, hopes, visions and social limitations. Thus, it can be difficult to see clearly how class background or gender affect an individual's possibilities. Things are not always well defined. If we focus on separate individuals, it is easy to find examples of people who do not follow the expected social patterns. At the same time, it is also possible to discern general social and cultural patterns, for example that men generally earn more money and have more influence than women do. Similarly, we can state that most people living in poorer big city neighbourhoods in Sweden have some type of immigrant background.

Structural obstacles are often identified using statistics and social scientific analyses. The patterns that can be discerned show, among other things, that it is difficult for an immigrant woman or a man with a working-class background to become director of a company. These structural obstacles not only constitute abstract statistics, but also have a crucial impact on people's inner worlds. They have an almost material effect on people's opportunities and identity projects. Such obstacles can manifest themselves in the form of values, attitudes, poor self-esteem, negative self-image or strategies of resistance. For example, a young man from a working-class family who is enrolled at a university may feel he is a fraud, despite the fact that he has been accepted into a prestigious course and is on his way to making an academic career. His poor self-esteem and experience of insufficiency – of not having the 'right' background – take over and become a real psychological obstacle.

Ove Sernhede's study of a group of young men with immigrant backgrounds and living in a poor neighbourhood in Gothenburg provides good examples of the global youth culture and of modern identity formation (Sernhede 2002). The young men he interviewed show a high degree of reflexivity. They analyse and critically scrutinize the social conditions that mark the circumstances under which they grew up. These young people have their backgrounds in Africa, Latin America and the Middle East. They have developed a strong loyalty to their neighbourhood, which is manifested, among other things, in the cultivation of a territorial mythology – a 'nationalism of the neighbourhood'. These young men identify themselves with the frustration, rage and anger that are given shape in the North American ghetto culture; they are influenced by American rap singers and gang films. It is through these filters that they 'read' their own childhood environment. They neither distance themselves from nor disparage the neighbourhood. Instead, they turn their energy and rage against the majority society. Their criticism is directed at those in power – politicians and heads of industry – and at Swedish society.

> Sweden doesn't need any apartheid laws; we don't need laws that force immigrants to live in certain areas. It's already the case that all the non-whites live separately, so it's just like it was in South Africa anyway. You understand man. So you could say that Hammarkullen or Hjällbo are like Gothenburg's Soweto ... but there's a difference – we don't have a Mandela. (Sernhede 1998: 26)

Like many American rap singers, these young men see themselves as neighbourhood soldiers, who have formed an ethnic alliance to combat repression. One keyword is 'respect'. Using cultural means of expression, they try to penetrate and elucidate societal repression. This struggle is pursued using symbols, artefacts, language and creative interpretation. The knowledge they value and use is not something they learned in school. These young men are elaborating their own rhetoric and making use of different types of popular culture to develop their own critical perspective.

Sernhede shows how these young men see through and relate critically to the legitimate culture, that is, the culture conveyed via the schools and in society. By seeking information, knowledge and material themselves, these young people are acting and reacting to social injustices and deficiencies in the societal system. This example reveals the functional dynamics between actor and structure as well as the prerequisites for real change. These young men are not only the victims of societal structures, but they are also actively trying to relate to their own social exclusion. In Nils Hammarén's studies we see how this kind of awareness is manifested in specific ways of relating to the relation between place, sexuality and gender. His study (Hammarén 2005) shows clearly that it can be difficult to talk about sexuality without placing such issues in a specific spatial and social context.

Identity as a Process

When we talk about young people in the public or in other contexts, words and concepts are often used that indicate change, flexibility, experimentation and searching. The period of youth stands for something positive, for energy, physicality, sexuality, vitality and the future – an ideal. If we consider, for example, cosmetic surgery and the exercise industry, it would seem that the search for youthfulness has become accentuated. Increasing numbers of people turn to doctors to achieve a more youthful appearance. However, for some young people, the teenage years entail a great deal of suffering. Many are unhappy and have problems with self-esteem; young women go on diets and develop eating disorders, and so on. The picture is quite complicated.

Today, many demands are placed on young people. They must succeed at school, fulfil social expectations and begin formulating the foundations of their own life. There is no general or universal regularity in how this will be manifested in practice. If we wish to study young people's paths into adult life, we must look more closely at how background factors such as class, gender and ethnicity vary and find different concrete manifestations. Childhood conditions vary, and this variability is expressed through a number of different identity projects.

I would like to return to the criticism directed at the developmental psychology paradigm at the beginning of this chapter. The following may be seen as a follow-up to my criticism of the developmental line of thought that has been inspired by psychoanalysis, but I also wish to point out certain ways in which we can develop the discussion on youth and identity. First, I would like to suggest how we could reinterpret and rethink certain central concepts and frames of understanding concerning youth.

- *Circular development.* It is possible, to a certain extent, to talk about linear development. Children and teenagers acquire an increasingly complex and adaptive ability to live in modern society. This development can be measured in terms of cognitive or emotional maturity. When we approach what is often called high-, but primarily post-adolescence, however, it is not as relevant to focus on maturity or psychological development. This sometimes long middle phase, stretching from the late teens to adulthood, can take on very different forms. To understand how young people's internal worlds are shaped during this time period, we need to use an arsenal of concepts that adequately capture the interplay between actors and structures. Today, it is becoming more difficult to find definite indicators of what may be viewed as, for example, an achieved identity or an identity that requires no further experimentation. Much of the developmental line of thought is based on the notion that there exists in each individual some type of permanent core or self. My suggestion is that we instead use a model that emphasizes interaction, interplay, flexibility and change. The identity is formed in relation to a relatively changeable surrounding world. Thus, psychological challenges do not come from within, but are instead constantly created through interaction with the environment. Our goals, prerequisites, possibilities and the playing field are not fixed. What we should be studying is how the internal and external worlds meet and how new constellations of mentality are constantly being created. This dynamic becomes very clear when we talk about sexuality. The construction of gender and sexuality always occurs in relation to a society in which there are normative, moral and political factors of influence.

- *Reflexive normativity.* As norms, values and attitudes change, we require a more flexible attitude towards society. Much of the developmental line of thought is characterized by a picture of society as static. Thus, according to this line of thought, it is the individual who must change, develop, mature and adapt to an established and stable society. This picture should be replaced by a more dynamic notion of changeable actors and structures. In this way, it would be more difficult to talk about normal sexual development or to establish stages that will lead to a mature adult identity. A reflexive attitude toward maturity, normality, morals and ethics implies wariness of establishing static pictures of what is normal.
- *Historical change.* There is no functioning universal theory of human beings, in any case not if our goal is to try to say something about young people's situation and identity in contemporary Western society. If we wish to study how young people form their identities, we should contextualize and historicize. But what does this entail? We can certainly identify and describe central processes and demands that are placed on today's young people. But such general descriptions and analyses must always be related to specific social and cultural contexts. Factors such as class, gender, ethnicity and place must be weighed into the analysis. It is also important to develop a historical sensibility. How is today's situation different from that of people who grew up in the 1960s? How are young people affected by the growth of new media, labour market changes, cultural ideals and other contemporary phenomena?

This book is primarily framed in a gender perspective. It deals with issues of gender, identity, sexuality and everyday life. This does not mean, however, that other perspectives or issues are peripheral. I have tried to discuss how young people create their gender identity within the framework of an everyday life that may be marked by various kinds of social exclusion or transgression or by a need to be normal. What we can see is that there are still many barriers and obstacles, despite young people's basically liberal attitudes towards their own potential to express their sexuality. Sexuality is never completely free – there are always rules to be followed. Even in cases when young people clearly break with conventions and what is most normal, they must still adhere to certain rules. They must also be prepared to encounter resistance and negative reactions from others. At the same time, however, we can see today how the male hegemony is being challenged and, thereby, also changed. In a society marked by an ideal of gender equality and a strong awareness of gender issues, the powers that be must adapt. It is no longer possible to exercise unequivocal male power; instead it is more a question of modifying claims to power and giving shape to more elastic forms of power. Just as Foucault points out in his book *The History of Sexuality* (1978, 1987a, 1987b), struggles against power are not fought outside, but instead within the field of power. This means, however, that power is never unambiguous, stable or even distinct.

Chapter 11

Epilogue: Cyberspace, Media and Sexuality

Throughout this book, the media are somehow present, but it is not always obvious in what ways and how they affect us. We find, in the media, an almost constant flow of images, ideas and notions of the body, sexuality, relations and ideals. It is possible, but not easy, to deal with all these images, and somehow they influence us. Everyday life is imbued with this flow of images and ideas. It has gradually become more difficult to create a distance or a space outside this flow.

However, even if we accept this idea of mediaization and 'a new reality', it is not easy to identify clear, observable changes in everyday life. In what ways are the young people studied in this book affected by this development, and does it really mean that their 'reality' has been totally transformed? Reading the literature on cyberspace and mediaization, one encounters an image of a totally transformed social and cultural reality. Obviously, there are some great exaggerations in much of this literature.

In this chapter, I will try to get closer to this discussion and draw some conclusions with respect to issues of youth, sexuality and mediaization. Although we are aware of how the media influence everyday life and the construction of identity and sexuality, it seems that young people's identity-formation is taking place somewhere 'outside' popular culture and the media sphere. However, this observation may be an effect of the difficulties inherent in detecting and studying media influences.

This chapter should be read as an elaboration on some of the perhaps less obvious tracks taken in this book. Taking its point of departure as a theoretical discussion on media and social reality, we gradually move closer to issues surrounding young people's construction of identity and sexuality. Whereas the content of Chapter 10 rounds off the previous chapters, this chapter is more a meditation on the central issues of mediaization and the construction of late-modern sexuality.

The first section introduces the overall topic of the chapter and situates it in the literature on mediaiziation. In the next part, we return to Jean Baudrillard. Thereafter follows a section on the metaphor of the cyborg. In the last sections, I discuss the relation between the Internet and the creation of neotribes. Finally, there is a section on reflexivity, where I begin my summary of the entire chapter.

Mediaization and Sexuality

At the beginning of the 1960s, Marshall McLuhan wrote his book *Understanding the Media: The Extension of Man* (1964). The book was highly acclaimed by critics and social scientists, and McLuhan was compared with Newton, Freud and Einstein. Instead of allowing himself to be hypnotized by media content, as many others had done, McLuhan made a radical claim – that *the medium is the message*. He meant, in other words, that the technology helped to influence and transform consciousness. Everything from perception to behaviour was affected by the new media. McLuhan talked about how the self was being stretched and how a global consciousness was being formed. McLuhan coined the expression *the global village*.

McLuhan was among the first to discuss the effects of mediaization. Naturally, the media landscape of the 1960s was completely different from that of today, yet the discussion McLuhan started is more relevant now than ever. Today, there is a rich and growing body of literature on the media, Internet, and on the new information technology and society. I do not intend to delve into all of these discussions, but will be content with addressing some of the most important questions – those directly tied to our discussion of sexuality and identity.

When browsing through the literature on how the new media technologies affect people, one comes across a mixture of utopias and dystopias. As the boundaries become increasingly shifting, it is sometimes difficult to differentiate between academic literature and pure science fiction. The core issue here concerns the extent to which the new media change the conditions for identity formation. If we assume that it is becoming more and more difficult, and perhaps impossible, to distinguish some forms of social reality from simulations – environments, relations and sensations created through media technology – then many of the philosophical and sociological categories that previously formed the basis for shaping our consciousness have ceased to apply.

For instance, Paul Virilio (1991, 2000), a French philosopher, claimed that people need no longer travel. They do not, in any case, need to use cars, trains or planes in order to take a journey. An individual can, in principle, sit in one room and simultaneously have contact with the entire world through his/her modem and computer. This person is at risk of becoming a stranger to his/her own body as well as to real human relationships – if such will exist at all in the future. The above could be a vision of the completely extended self, one lacking points of reference and stable roots. This implies, by extension, that an entirely new perception of reality and a new human being are developing. Perhaps we can no longer use terms such as self, ego and identity.

Our social and cultural reality is obviously changing. But how much and in what ways are people affected? Looking back at the Swedish investigation into young people's sexual lives, it is not clear how the media influence sexuality. But before drawing any conclusions, I will return to the French philosopher Jean Baudrillard and present more of his theoretical contributions to this discussion.

The Prophet of the Cyber People

A man, around 65 years of age, is at a new age festival and reading one of his own philosophical reflections on contemporary life – *Chance: Three Days in the Desert*. The scene is a casino and the man is Jean Baudrillard:

> Over the sound of the slot machines being played and the occasional jackpot being won, the disparate group of listeners strains to catch what he is saying through his heavily accented English. 'Chaos' sounds like 'cows', 'bodies' like 'birdies'. Later in the evening, he will return to recite one of his poems, 'Motel Suicide', backed by a rock band and wearing a gold lamé suit. (Butler 1991: 1)

Baudrillard (see also Chapter 2) has – as earlier mentioned – received considerable attention and criticism for his relatively abstruse and challenging theories on contemporary society. He has pursued a number of theses that have caused the hair of most sociologists and social scientists to stand on end. He argued, among other things, that we live in a society that has moved beyond all of the social distinctions and categories that have formed the basis for our discussions on societal development during the 20th century.

What is reality? Is it actually possible to talk about such a notion? Baudrillard's project largely concerns questioning our predominant conceptions of reality, particularly what is sociology's object of interest – social reality. The upshot is that many sociologists have found it difficult to digest his views that the social dimension is dead and that classic social scientific categories and variables, such as class, gender and ethnicity, have lost their significance in postmodernity. The question is, what does Baudrillard mean when he questions the impact of social factors? His statements and theoretical notions can appear unrealistic and unscientific. His claims are never based on actual studies of the matter at hand, but he has instead devoted himself to theoretical speculation about the present.

Baudrillard differentiated between three historical periods and related these to the Renaissance, the early industrial age and the current postmodern era (Baudrillard 1983). These three periods entail a gradual intensification of what he called *simulation*. When the feudal system broke down, and the sovereign's total power was questioned, an opening was also created for interpretations, ambiguities and shifts in symbolic meaning. During this initial phase, signs and symbols were being liberated from their material attributes. Increasing *arbitrariness* was gradually created, that is, symbols could be used to designate a number of different phenomena and the previously strong symbolic order was demolished step by step. During this first period, people still respected the pristine; they tried to imitate 'the natural'. This was the great epoch of the theatre.

When we enter the industrial age, we find a completely different order. Here the signs had multiplied and lost their material attributes. The language system was becoming increasingly autonomous. Whereas one had earlier tried to create images of humans – for example mechanical representations (automatons) – the products created at this time were instead characterized by their own logic. The robot was certainly modelled after humans, but it was also largely an autonomous product of the industrial system. It was now possible to mass-produce artefacts. The original and 'genuine' had lost its meaning as the basis for this process. During this epoch, the distinction between some kind of reality and the language system, or between referents and codes, gradually ceased to apply.

At this point, we enter the third period. Now the dissolution of meaning that started during the second period has begun to accelerate. It is no longer reality that determines people's construction of the world, but instead the model. Baudrillard received considerable inspiration from McLuhan's phrase 'the media is the message'. It is the form per se that guides communication. Thus, the mediaization of society has drastic consequences for how people interact and shape their own reality.

Perhaps Baudrillard's most interesting work is when he compares Disneyland and the USA, or Watergate and the USA. According to him, it is no longer possible to say that Disneyland is a product of the imagination that has little to do with reality. If anything, the distinction between Disneyland, where illusions and dreams are actively created, and the USA in general lost its meaning. Given this line of reasoning, Watergate was not an exception, but instead merely an illustration of the corruption, greed and autocratic ways that are spreading throughout the USA (Baudrillard 1990).

In the postmodern landscape, it is no longer possible to differentiate between good and evil or between reality and illusion. We have moved beyond these types of classic markers and distinctions. Everything we thought had meaning, any significance at all, has now lost its meaning. This is particularly true of the physical and the sexual. The more this sphere of intimacy is exploited and explored, using all possible means, the emptier it becomes. Sexuality and religion have lost their ability to charge our existence, to give rise to ecstasy and mystery. Thereby, everyday life has also been emptied of much of its original significances and of meaning making.

However, as we have seen in this book, young people still attach notable meaning to sexuality and feelings. Today we can observe considerable creativity and activity in the youth culture. Although many young people feel controlled by restrictive norms and values, they also tend to crossover and create new ways of expressing their sexuality. The ways of creating meaning and of attaching feelings to things and people sometimes seem endless.

Life in postmodern society has become increasingly uncertain, that is, there are no longer any self-evident traditions or rules for living on which one can fall back. The more people try to escape this uncertain existence, the more it is formed and reproduced. Yet we can no longer talk about alienation. Western society has moved beyond alienation, as there is no longer anything from which to be alienated. In late-modern society, there is great acceptance for pluralism, ambiguity and ambivalence, but at the same time new intolerances are being created. For instance, Baudrillard claimed that tolerance leads to increased difficulty in expressing disgust with something, which in turn causes disgust. We are suddenly disgusted with this lack of disgust – our reaction to a scarcity of reactions.

When Baudrillard made his journey through the USA – a country for which he seems to feel both love and hate – he observed a complete dissolution of society and a loss of meaning making. He saw how America was spread out like a wasteland, devoid of meaning and symbolic charges. All distinctions have collapsed in postmodernity. Transvestites question all gender distinctions, the media form politics, and war is enacted and settled primarily on the TV screen. If it comes to the worst, Baudrillard's ruthless dissection of the analysis categories we are used to employing when observing social life leaves us, in the end, without any understanding of society whatsoever.

As we well know, social reality is complex. Maybe there are some truths in what Baudrillard is saying. But just as we can detect signs of mediaization, a changing reality and simulations, there are also many signs indicating the opposite – new ways of creating meaning, of making community work and of constructing rather stable identities. Baudrillard presents an image of the post-emotional society, but at the same time there is a considerable amount of evidence for the existence of a therapeutic and emotional society. In contemporary Western society, people talk a lot, work with their emotional problems and care about how they feel and live their lives.

The Cyborg – A Feminist?

The film *Blade Runner* (1982), directed by Ridley Scott, has become something of a classic in the genre of future scenarios and cyborgs (a complex combination of machine and human). We can follow the main character, played by Harrison Ford, on his hunt for subversive cyborgs. The setting is a large futuristic city, populated by people and their very advanced playthings. Here we can only begin to predict the threat from thinking machines that is fully elaborated in other films, such as *The Terminator* (1984). What makes cyborgs interesting is their close resemblance to humans. These films reveal a boundary so fragile that, in the end, it is difficult to determine who is a human and who is a machine. This is illustrated in the final scenes of the later version of *Blade Runner*, when we learn that even the character played by Harrison Ford is a cyborg – the boundaries have ceased to apply.

The cyborg has become something of the admass society's root metaphor, that is, a metaphor that comprises several central aspects of contemporary society. This metaphor functions superbly as a tight and composite picture of the extended and nearly extinguished self. It blurs the boundaries between nature and culture, man and machine, reality and illusion. And, given that it is useful in pointing out a number of boundary transgressions, it also functions well as a guide in the current, postmodern state of things.

In her now classic essay 'A Cyborg Manifesto' (1990), the American feminist and historian Donna Haraway stressed precisely these boundary-transgressing qualities. She wished to designate the cyborg as a symbol for contemporary gender politics. The cyborg does not respect the boundaries between masculinity and femininity. Here there is no original gender and no essence. In contrast to many other culture critics, who have seen the origins of culture crisis in technological development,

Haraway tried to illustrate how technology can show the way out of oppression and help to form entirely new identities.

The cyborg's complete disinterest in establishing a principal interpretive framework for the whole of reality indicates an increasingly pluralized world. The metaphor is well suited to a feminism that wishes to withdraw from the gender-polarized universe that previous generations of feminists helped to reinforce, but the question is how far one can stretch this metaphor? A fairly far-fetched dissolution of the boundaries of gender and self are probably not desirable. Yet this is the origin of all change. The question, however, is whether the complete obliteration of all boundaries is to be desired. What happens, then, to ethics, morals, love and politics? By way of conclusion, Haraway (1990: 223) wrote the following about the cyborg:

> Cyborg imagery can suggest a way out of the maze of dualisms in which we have explained our bodies and our tools to ourselves. This is a dream not of a common language, but of a powerful infidel heteroglossia. It is an imagination of a feminist speaking in tongues to strike fear into the circuits of the super savers of the New Right. It means both building and destroying machines, identities, categories, relationships, spaces, stories. Although both are bound in a spiral dance, I would rather be a cyborg than a goddess.

Towards the end of *Terminator 2* (1991), the cyborg, played by Arnold Schwarzenegger, destroys himself by sinking into a sea of molten metal. The terminator realized this was the only way to protect humanity from what would otherwise happen in the future – the cyborgs would take over and destroy humanity. The question is, however, whether the cyborg is such a promising metaphor for change and for a better society?

Haraway's works are very close to the whole genre of poststructuralist feminist literature. Many of the works presented here are also clearly influenced by writers such as Haraway, Judith Butler and Judith Halberstam. Some of the phenomena presented in the different studies – for example political lesbians and bisexual young men – could be seen as part of the 'queering' of everyday life. The critique of binary positions and of the classical gender dualism is now a part of day-to-day existence. Therefore, the cyborg works rather perfectly as a symbol for the new generation of media-saturated and alternative sexual identities.

Internet and Neotribes

There is no doubt that the evolution of the Internet has entailed great changes in how people communicate. The question is how great? In discussions on modern information technology it sometimes sounds as though the conditions for formation of a self have changed completely. Enthusiasts can go overboard and draw too far-reaching conclusions based on the fact that, today, many people spend a considerable amount of time at their computer connected to the Internet. A classic pattern – new technology leads to new forms of moral panic or indignation – is repeated.

The American psychologist Sherry Turkle (1996) has conducted a number of studies on how people's use of computers and the Internet affects their self-perception. Her studies show, naturally enough, that it is impossible to draw general conclusions concerning these phenomena. Certainly there are young people who become dependent on the computer. Turkle showed how several individuals used Internet chat as a way to solve problems; they felt a certain security in being anonymous, in talking as and with a stranger; this made it easier for some people to open up and share sensitive issues. Perhaps this is positive to a certain extent, but for some of Turkle's informants the computer had become a drug; they were, in principle, connected to the Internet all the time.

But what is it that technology changes? We see how the same types of human behaviour normally observed in everyday life are now spreading on the Internet: love, infidelity, friendship, sexuality, collecting and all manner of passions. What constitutes the difference? The individuals we encounter on the Internet are often anonymous; they have no faces, bodies or odours, and they do not care about appearances or, for that matter, about gender. Much of what has previously guided our everyday interactions – particularly all our real face-to-face meetings with people – has virtually vanished in cyberspace.

In his book *Microserfs*, Douglas Coupland described how one of the main characters – Michael – meets a woman (?): 'BarCode eats flat food, too. And she-*slash*-he's written a Flatlander *Oop!*-style product with immense game potential. BarCode is my soulmate. There is only one person for me out there, and I have found it. BarCode's my ally in this world *and* ...' (Coupland 1996: 323). There is enormous freedom in not being bound to a body, in being spared all of one's bodily defects and irritants. The question is, however, what happens when the non-physical relation is forced into the light of social reality – when the two individuals must meet face to face? Perhaps at this point the cyberworld enters a harsh reality where appearance is crucial and where the body establishes a certain framework for the interaction.

The Internet does, however, imply great opportunities to meet people with similar interests. Yet the type of public emerging from the Internet assumes somewhat different forms than those of the ordinary public. The groups that emerge are sometimes short-lived; they arise and disappear at a uniform rate. Perhaps, in the end, it is only because there actually exists a relation between the Internet and social reality that interest groups or organizations are maintained over time. These *neotribes*, that is, collective groupings arising occasionally on the Internet, appear to be dependent on their ability to materialize in some way – otherwise they lose their power to attract young people.

The notion of the totally extended self – a person who, via his/her computer, lives on the Internet – is still just an illusion. Probably only a small number of individuals would be judged, on the basis of current conditions, as highly deviant. The Internet has partly changed the conditions for formation of the self, but rather than discussing a total change, we should study how the individual adds something by using this technological and informational system. Thus far, the notion that a self could be formed solely on the Internet is absurd.

However, looking at the young people in our study, the Internet has clearly become part of everyday life and sexuality. The Internet is used to chat, meet new people, view pornography, contact different sexual communities, and so on. In many cases, the Internet has contributed to greater freedom in relating to and meeting friends and lovers. But there are obviously also great risks involved. There are incidents in which adults try to take advantage of young people's use of the Internet as a way of finding sexual partners. Among other things, we find organized paedophile leagues and other treacherous communities in cyberspace.

Mediaization – A Journey Towards Life's Absolute Zero?

On a stage, a woman is allowing a plastic surgeon to operate on her. Yet this is not normal cosmetic surgery. This woman has not engaged the surgeon to operate on her skin and face in order to attain the most desirable facial features or the most beautiful body. This is about art. The artist Orlan has engaged the surgeon to work according to her own instructions. She is creating a work of art from her own body. Orlan has arranged to have the operation filmed, so it can be followed step by step. We can watch while Orlan sculptures her own body and creates a unique work of art. Her body suddenly belongs to the whole world. It is there to be viewed – to be an object of fascination – as a *global body*.

According to Joshua Meyrowitz (1985), the dividing line between the private and the public has shifted and is sometimes rubbed out. What was previously a relatively stable boundary has been transformed into a permeable membrane. The private, which previously took place in 'the back regions' only – the bedroom, bathroom or other private places – is now trickling out and leaking in to people watching TV. Because the camera can register the smallest facial expression, every glance and body movement, it is difficult to maintain a distance and to present oneself in a completely satisfactory way. If one, during a live broadcast, says something wrong or happens to burp, these mistakes must be lived with.

Today there is a fascination with people's private lives – a longing to tear down boundaries and to see what is happening behind the scenes. We can see that the self is being transformed through the media and that this is manifested in particular ways. Presentation of the self is a focal point of contemporary culture. The media's ability to zoom in and focus on details also serves to change people's perceptions. The technology is changing and helping to create conditions for a changed perception and, with time, another self. These changes concern the complex self.

The assumption that people of today have ceased to move in a social space or have lost themselves in an imaginary world is a radical one. Even if the self is extended, we must nevertheless ask what this implies for the social individual, for the interplay that still takes place in everyday life – in a fairly concrete social reality. The fact that people are influenced daily by media and formulate their thoughts in categories supplied by the media does not automatically imply that the media have taken control over human existence. Yet the media's effects on perception and thought are considerable. The self is extended a little at a time. The question is how much extension can take place without the risk of dissolution and destruction?

The extended self takes shape at the point of intersection of modern information technology and media, on the one side, and people's self-formation and bodies, on the other. Certain conceptions are challenged and some new ways of viewing humankind are created. The body, for example, assumes a partly new and more peripheral significance. But this is only true of certain media. On TV and in entertainment programmes, for instance, the body is instead in focus. Here we observe a tribute to the beautiful and well-trained body. Yet information technology is affecting our attitude toward the body and the self in various ways.

Recently, a new show has appeared on TV – *The Sex Inspectors*. There is already a Swedish version of this show. Couples are asked to talk about and act out their sexual 'problems', whereupon the inspectors give advice and even show how these couples can achieve a more sexually satisfying life. Thus, the experts are now even present in our bedrooms.

The Media and Self-Formation

The media help to increase reflexivity. This, however, does not automatically imply increased levels of knowledge or better readiness to manage one's life. It is possible to differentiate between different types of reflexivity. Perhaps the most common is *instrumental reflexivity*, which contributes to the development of a kind of everyday commonsense. Through this type of reflexivity, individuals learn to fit in and to avoid breaking too radically with general cultural patterns. Above all they learn codes and rules for how one should behave in certain situations. Experience with media and good knowledge of popular culture and other media phenomena are part of the formation of cultural capital. This type of knowledge constitutes an important complement to academic knowledge. A person who is not familiar with the Beatles, Madonna, Mel Gibson, Julia Roberts, MTV, Microsoft or other predominant media people or companies is viewed as rather odd. Today, many of our everyday topics of conversation are taken from the media.

Normative reflexivity is narrower in purpose. We learn how we *should* think and behave via the media. There are strong normative elements in everything from news reports to films. Media scholars have discussed in depth the fact that there are predominant messages in the media and that these are usually tied to claims to power. Stuart Hall (1999) distinguished among three different attitudes toward the media: the predominating, the negotiating and the oppositional position.

Assuming the *predominating position* is equivalent to displaying a lack of a critical attitude toward TV or newspapers. The *negotiating position* implies that the individual partly accepts much of the news as truths, but that he/she can simultaneously engage in critical observation. Finally, the *oppositional position* implies that the individual is primarily highly critical of that which is presented as objective news or truths. This attitude is characterized by the *hermeneutics of suspicion* and by a state of constant doubt.

In the West, people are washed over by media material. If they do not try to relate to this flow, the risk is great that certain messages will be transformed into truths. This concerns, for example, how gender and sexuality is presented in the media. It is still the case that men and women are portrayed in a stereotyped fashion, although there certainly are exceptions. The fact that we are exposed from an early age to programmes and films depicting men and women as completely different beings must affect how we view gender. This is true of many other phenomena as well. To a great extent, the media reflect the patterns of power and the super- and subordination that exist in a society. At the same time, of course, there are opportunities to break with the general and the normative. The media also open up the intermediate area of the imagination.

It is here, in this intermediate area, that utopian reflexivity is found – where thoughts on alternative lifestyles and ways of life are born. In this utopian zone, where boundaries are transgressed, there is scope in which to dream, fantasize, and formulate ideas about a different life. This area has traditionally been the domain of art, where people have been allowed to consider and fantasize about things they feel cannot be acted out in everyday life. The media create openings for experimenting with identities and for hybridity, that is, for the complex combination of different types of identities. By developing an intermediate area in which the stable is dissolved into a number of different hybrid forms, the media serve to produce dream worlds. They open a direct channel to the unconscious and stimulate the imagination. Aspects of life that were previously distinct are united, and traditional distinctions are broken up and vanish. This media world and these dream worlds also emerge from social reality; they derive their nourishment from this reality and are therefore eternally united with and dependent on it.

It is no longer possible to make simple distinctions between an imaginary and a social reality. They have collapsed and drifted into each other. The importance of place has partially decreased. Today, it is easy to communicate over great distances. We can imagine that a digital city could be a reality – that increasing numbers of social institutions will be located on and managed via the Internet. People will meet in cyberspace instead of in a social reality. People need their dream worlds, but they also live in a reality filled with trivial social encounters and events. There would seem to be no doubt that objects, things, people, bodies and worn-out greetings still have meaning. Yet the world of things has been filled with entirely new objects – album covers, videos, CDs, games, old computers, classic feature films and much more. For many, this universe of popular culture is of great emotional importance. It is here that meaning is created.

Today, we also find an increasing fascination for everyday life. This is manifested in the countless number of soap operas and reality programmes shown on TV. The desire to penetrate people's intimate places and to watch their behaviour, emotions and facial expressions has increased. Fascination with the everyday could be interpreted as a sign of the spreading of a blasé attitude – a kind of search for experiences that stir us up and create a feeling of being affected. Thomas Ziehe (1989) discussed the notion of *potentiation*, that is, of a longing for charging one's life with intensive emotional experiences.

What, then, has changed? One can imagine that the media logic has, to an increasing extent, influenced the interaction patterns of day-to-day life. This could be manifested, for example, in the importance of being seen and of being visual. This could be a question of having a beautiful and well-trained body – a body shaped at the gym and sometimes through plastic surgery. Being media smart is equivalent to functioning in a world increasingly permeated by a media logic. Lifestyles, identities and images of the self are created, circulated and upheld in the media. 'I'm seen, therefore I am.' This could be a question of having the right lifestyle, which can be manifested through a particular style of dress, attitude and spatial positioning; in other words, the individual must move in the right crowds and frequent the right clubs. The high degree of reflexivity characterizing much of the interplay and encounters between people also leads to constant self-scrutiny. How should one behave and dress to be perceived as correct? This type of question is related to how factors such as class, gender and ethnicity intersect one another and create a background for many patterns of consumption.

The mediaization of everyday life has a number of consequences for how we approach and discuss questions of identity development and sexuality in late-modern society. Roughly speaking, we can discern three different consequences of mediaization: the structuring of everyday life, the questioning of both social distinctions and hegemonic demands. Paradoxically enough, this development leads both to increased chances for questioning the predominant social order and, in some respects, to the reinforcement of this order.

The structuring of everyday life occurs largely with regard to mass media use. Today, individuals have every opportunity to design a pattern of media use that fits the lifestyles they have developed. The increased selection of different media and the possibilities for combining them allow for great individualization of media use. At the same time, more and more identity spaces are created and we see an increased dependence on the media. A structure is developed in everyday life that revolves around certain television programmes, series, computer games or whatever else is of interest to people and shapes their lives.

Because it is possible to study other people's experiences and worlds, there is also more scope for the illusory transgression of boundaries. Meyrowitz (1985) pointed out how the media have helped to pull down different cultural barriers. This change need not, of course, result in real change, but there is always the possibility that it will. Perhaps it is the case that the media give people's dreams and desires the nourishment necessary for them to initiate action and change. The transformations pointed out by Meyrowitz have changed the prerequisites for modern-day identity formation. But if we are to address how these structuring processes affect people's perceptions and actions, we must also take into account the reception process per se.

Originally written in the 1970s, Stuart Hall's encoding/decoding model (1999) is a simple mental diagram that still works as a point of departure for discussions on and analyses of the media's influence on human thinking and behaviour. Even if the processes described by Meyrowitz have resulted in a general questioning of many social distinctions, they are, in the end, a matter of how individuals choose to approach a given text and how they assimilate and interpret various representations and images. In many respects, we still think and act within the confines of certain predominant conceptions about how society should be organized, about the relations between different social groups, and about specific configurations of power. At the same time, however, doubt is constantly being cast upon these configurations and the struggle over how we should create a good society is ongoing.

People's stories about themselves and the reflexive formation of an identity take place more and more within the framework of a mediaized society and everyday life. The media do not merely fill these stories with content, but they even help to structure people's existence. To a greater degree than in the past, contemporary biographies and novels are filled with references to popular culture and to the mediaized reality. Today, in order to talk about identity at all, we must be able to come closer to and understand people's great involvement in the popular culture. In the modern world of fiction, we meet individuals who are obsessed with and quite knowledgeable about popular culture. In order to understand these characters, it is necessary to master the art of intertextuality and to have the same knowledge. For example, how – without this knowledge – are we to understand Nick Hornby's character when he compares his new love to Susan Dey: 'Marie is pretty, in a cross-eyed American sort of way – she looks like a plumper version of Susan Dey, after *The Partridge Family* but before *L.A. Law* – if you're going to launch into a spontaneous and meaningless love affair you could do much worse' (Hornby 1995: 57).

Unfortunately, I am not able to present good answers to all the questions raised in this chapter. I believe there are some considerable difficulties involved in researching the connection between everyday life, sexuality and what we have called mediaization. However, I will try to end this chapter by drawing some preliminary conclusions.

The media and popular culture can be seen as a social and cultural space, filled with images, ideas and notions of the good life. I would say that young people collect and consume some of this imaginary material and also use it to create their identity and sexuality. We have seen how conceptions of love, sexuality, relations, emotions and gender are being transformed today. Many of the categories we once accepted as truths have been destabilized. Lina Paulsson (2005), for example, shows how heterosexual love is saturated with and partly constructed on the basis of media images of happy couples. Mediaization means that we can no longer draw a clear boundary between social reality and media images. What is 'real'?

Today, pornographic material is part of everyday life. Young people learn how to 'have sex' and how to perform and construct gender. But they are not in any way slaves to the media or just passive victims. Instead, they have learned how to relate to and use media in everyday life. But they are not active and creative all the time. A great deal of media use is just for pleasure; it is something you do to kill time and have fun.

The boundaries between what we call social everyday life and the media have become more vague and unclear. Young people live inside the media, and their reality is imbued with a constant flow of images and ideas. This new situation creates challenges for researchers and others interested in these questions.

PART V
Appendix

Chapter 12

Method and Methodology

· **Investigation Plan and Structure**

Much of the discussion found in the present book is based on results from a major Swedish investigation of how young people do gender, identity and sexuality. Yet our aim has also been to take a broad approach and to tie these results to a more international discussion. The international elements primarily consist of references to and discussions of Anglo-Saxon studies in the same area. We have also tried to include, as far as possible, comparison data from the Spanish-speaking parts of the world. It is evident that, in different parts of the world, scholars are obtaining similar results and seeing similar patterns. It is quite clear, too, that the same types of discussions about young people's sexuality are being pursued. At the same time, however, there are also rather significant differences. The present investigation deals primarily with how young people in the wealthier parts of the world are tackling these questions. Thus, we have not dealt with many of the social problems faced by young people in large parts of the world's poorer regions. It would, of course, be desirable to conduct such an investigation, as a contrast to the present one. The focus of the book – on the world's more privileged young people – allows us to present a rather hopeful picture of young people's social and cultural reality. Having said this, we wish to stipulate again that our description only applies to one part of a larger global reality.

Roughly speaking, the Swedish investigation comprises two parts: a survey study and qualitative in-depth studies. The original design was as follows:

1. *Phase 1. A survey study.* This was a survey of a representative sample of Swedish young people in the age range 15–18 years. As shown in the section below, this ambition was eventually modified. The purpose of this part of the investigation was to capture more general patterns. The survey questions dealt with everything from views on love, fidelity and gender equality to pornography and homosexuality. Another purpose was that the survey would provide the basis for later selection of a number of interesting groups that we could study using qualitative methods.
2. *Phase 2. Qualitative in-depth studies.* Our intention was to study a number of groups of young people that could, in different ways, help to form a more complete picture of how factors such as class, gender, ethnicity and sexuality interact and create certain cultural patterns. The doctoral students working within the framework of the project have studied, in different ways, how these types of social and cultural points of intersection may lead to different

outcomes. We will account for the various in-depth studies below. In order to broaden the picture somewhat during the course of the investigation, we have engaged students and scholars working on other studies in this area. Thus, the qualitative part of the investigation involves researchers tied to the project as well as a number of individuals who have participated by writing book chapters or by working on the project for shorter periods of time.

The advantage of this type of design is that we obtain both an overall picture and a more complex and in-depth picture of the contemporary youth culture. At the same time, however, we have encountered a number of methodological questions and problems that we have had to solve during the course of the investigation. Below is a discussion of two questions we have discussed and then chosen to solve in the following manner:

1. We decided at a rather early stage not to use statistical data to study and analyse some issues, for example how class, sex and ethnicity interact in the construction of gender. We saw that a statistical approach would entail the great risk of reducing the complexity of the picture and, worse, of helping to create stereotypes. For instance, it proved to be difficult to categorize and group the data into the informant types 'Swedes' versus 'immigrants'. Regardless of how we defined the categories, the result was always unsatisfactory. The available data were also inadequate with regard to classifying parental occupation. Many young people found it difficult to specify their parents' occupations. This shows the problems inherent in creating variables to cover more complex phenomena. We do not mean that it is impossible to work with statistics in this way, just that we could not solve this 'problem' satisfactorily. We chose, therefore, to work with more modest and 'simpler' statistics.
2. Selection of in-depth studies. Our aim was to choose a number of strategic groups of young people on the basis of the survey data. However, this approach is insufficient in terms of the flexibility required in this type of investigation. We have instead chosen to let the survey data give us ideas and thoughts about possible appropriate samples. We have then sought groups that are able to reflect how the above-mentioned factors may help to form contemporary identities. Moreover, we have chosen to combine this strategy with spontaneous selection, that is, when opportunities have arisen, we have involved scholars and students in writing about specific and exciting case studies.

Our different approaches and decisions have resulted in a research design marked by a combination of a selective and well-planned selection strategy and a flexible and more spontaneous selection strategy. In the sections below, we will first describe the survey procedure and then present, in more detail, the in-depth studies that have formed the basis of the present investigation. Finally, we will return to more general issues concerning the study's outcomes and results.

The Survey Study

Our book includes data from a major survey study conducted (autumn 2000/spring 2001) within the framework of the project *Youth, Gender and Sexuality in the Borderland* (*Ungdom, kön och sexualitet i gränslandet*) and funded by HSFR (the Swedish Council for Research in the Humanities and Social Sciences) and FAS (the Swedish Council for Working Life and Social Research). The initial aim was to carry out the survey using a representative sample of the Swedish population and to focus on a number of different age groups within the category *youth*. The aim was modified with time, not least due to practical and financial circumstances, and ended up focusing on two different cities: Gothenburg and Kalmar. The choice was a natural one, as project members had their homes in one or the other of these two cities. By choosing a big city and a smaller city, we felt we could capture several of the variables influencing young people's construction of sexuality and gender. Gothenburg, with its postmodern, globalized and differentiated nature, and Kalmar, with its somewhat more local nature, constituted a varied field for our investigation.

In this book, we have chosen to present data both from students in their third year of high school and from the whole sample (in the chapter on pornography). The high schools in Gothenburg were chosen partly to obtain samples from schools in the city centre and outlying areas, and partly to obtain a representative sample of all study programs. Thus, we also have a division based on vocational, practical programmes versus academic, theoretical programmes. Using statistics describing the catchment areas of the high schools, we were able to confirm our selection criteria with respect to class. Statistics on school performance, interruption of studies and absenteeism also helped us in the process of selecting high schools. In Kalmar, it was perhaps more difficult to capture the breadth of class variation and socially high- to low-status areas that are found in big cities. Thus, the high schools were chosen with respect to study programme: practical versus theoretical. However, in contrast to the Gothenburg study, many of the students in the Kalmar study came from small towns, giving us variation with regard to urban vs. rural background.

The study is based on a survey consisting of 138 questions. The questions deal with home and family conditions, social background, contentment with school/life, self-image, views on one's own body, sexual habits, attitudes, beliefs about other young people's sexual experiences as well as a battery of questions about crime and punishment. In particular focus are questions concerning sexual morals, self-image, gender and attitudes. A focus on the preventative and medical aspects of young people's sexuality is relatively common in similar studies, which is why we chose to look primarily at the cultural and social dimensions.

During the initial stage, we contacted the involved authorities to obtain permission to conduct the investigation. This sometimes proved to be a tricky undertaking, as several authorities and individuals needed to give their consent. Many times the wills of these parties did not coincide. Sometimes the school declined participation owing to the sensitive nature of the subject. This was particularly true of schools with high proportions of immigrant students. Sometimes the reasons were lack of time, being tired of surveys or that the study would disrupt students' schoolwork. On one occasion, two school nurses reacted negatively to questions on, for example anal sex, saying that such questions might 'legitimize such behaviour' or awaken the issue. One school nurse felt, for example, that we 'should protect students from questions about anal sex'. One teacher thought the survey violated students' privacy to an extreme degree, and another threw the surveys in the wastebasket. Things often went more smoothly in Kalmar, where only the consent of the municipality and the respective school principals was required. Yet even some schools in Kalmar declined to participate.

When we were finally authorized, we went out into the schools. This process was somewhat different in the different settings. In Kalmar, someone from the project visited the school and the class, described the purpose of the investigation, distributed the survey in the classroom and later collected the completed forms. In Gothenburg, due to lack of time/staff shortage, we let the teachers distribute the survey to their pupils. This, however, did not work particularly well, as we had no control over the surveys and the teachers were hesitant about handing out such sensitive material to the students. They felt uncomfortable and were uncertain as to how students would react to the questions. For this reason, we began visiting the participating schools ourselves. The students could now feel more secure, knowing there would be no middleman between them and us. In this way, our promise of confidentiality and anonymity could more easily be kept. Now there was no risk that someone other than a project member might read the survey answers.

The above-mentioned problems constitute ethical questions. We realized early on that we must change our approach in order to ensure respondents' privacy as well as to succeed in completing the survey study. On the whole, we have stressed issues of an ethical character both in the applications for permission to conduct the investigation and in our description of the project for the students, teachers and parents. A study of sexuality delves into areas that are private and sensitive. Thus, protecting the privacy of participants is essential. For this reason, the survey was conducted anonymously, and all personal information was removed in reports and articles. We additionally stressed that participation was voluntary, but also that a high participation rate was important. In this regard, however, the classroom situation would seem to be problematic. We cannot rule out the possibility that a few students who would rather not have participated felt forced to do so owing to peer pressure. We are well aware of this problem, but we have, at the same time, tried to minimize it by stressing the voluntary nature of the study. It may have occurred, however, that certain students who did participate felt violated by the sensitive and detailed questions posed in the survey. We tried to reduce students' misgivings through introductory texts in the survey and through our efforts to convey a tolerant and realistic view on questions of sexuality. A pilot study was conducted in the spring of 2000 with four classes. Here students were given the opportunity to comment on the survey. Their reactions were remarkably positive. We did, however, revise the survey somewhat prior to the main investigation.

Because all students present in the classroom responded to the survey (100% response frequency), any attrition is due to student absence on that day. A couple of students in every class were either ill, truant or engaged in other school activities, for example at theatre practice or working in a special education group. Several simply did not attend class, knowing that participation was voluntary. After counting dropouts, we estimate that 80% of students in the classes we visited completed the survey. This participation rate must be viewed as fairly good. On a few occasions, however, only part of the class showed up, owing to the above-mentioned reasons. In most cases, we had been informed of these absences prior to the meeting. To compensate for this attrition, we simply visited new classes until we were satisfied with the number of completed surveys. Naturally, this method implies certain problems of bias, but was the only simple solution in these cases. In one case, the teacher had selected students from the class when she knew we would be coming. In this way, she allowed some students to get out of responding so that the sample would better represent the entire class in terms of sex and ethnic background.

In total, 650 surveys have been collected, of which 418 (64%) come from high schools in Gothenburg and 232 (36%) from high schools in Kalmar. Of the 650 students, 294 (45%) are young men and 354 (55%) young women. That the total number of young men and women is only 648 (not 650) is due to internal attrition. The overall survey study, which also includes elementary school students, consists of a total of 1,331 completed surveys.

In the text, we present only simple statistical relationships; more complicated analyses have been postponed. In presenting the data in tabular form, we have set the level of significance at 0.05. The Chi square value indicates the possible relationships between different variables. If this value exceeds 0.05, we may reject the hypothesis that the relationship is statistically significant.

The Qualitative In-Depth Studies

The qualitative in-depth studies have been initiated and organized in a number of different ways. By way of introduction, we will provide an overview of the structure as well as brief descriptions of the in-depth studies. The aim of the project has been to try to obtain a good picture of how young people in different environments, with different social and cultural backgrounds, construct and create gender. We have chosen, therefore, a strategy of having, as a foundation, a permanent project staff working, over extended periods, on dissertation projects directed at specific youth groups. These doctoral students have received part of their funding through the project. The next staff category includes researchers who have worked, for shorter periods, with data collection. This has mostly been a question of a few months of funding. The aim of these studies has been to examine more closely a specific group. Moreover, a number of students have been involved in the project. They have written essays and often articles tied to the project. These activities, however, have not been funded. Finally, a number of people have been contacted for the sole purpose of writing papers for project anthologies.

The following section provides summary information about each subproject. This is intended to help the reader form an understanding of the empirical data underlying the discussions pursued in the book.[1]

Dissertation Projects

Within the framework of the project, three dissertation projects have received partial funding. The aim of these projects has been to capture the more fundamental changes occurring in youth culture, particularly with regard to how ethnic affiliation, class and gender create certain circumstances for the formation of sexuality. Below is a short description of these projects:

1. *Masculinity, ethnicity and identity* (Nils Hammarén, PhD in social work). The project's aim is to analyse how young men who have immigrant backgrounds and live in multicultural urban areas develop and create attitudes toward sexuality and identity (n=40).
2. *Young immigrant women, sexuality and identity* (Margareta Forsberg, PhD in social work). This is a parallel project to Hammarén's. The focus here, however, is on studying how young women with immigrant backgrounds deal with questions of gender, ethnicity and sexuality. This dissertation uses empirical data from both the survey and the interviews (n=24).
3. *Masculinity, sport and sexuality* (Jesper Andreasson, PhD in sociology). The empirical data for this dissertation consists of two case studies of athletic clubs. The focus here is on male handball players (n=20) and female soccer players (n=14). The data comprise both interviews and participant observations.

The first two projects form the foundation of the present chapters on sexuality and the multicultural society. Andreasson's study of female soccer players plays an important role in the chapter on young masculinity. This study allows us to reflect on the question of what masculinity is, could be or often becomes.

Focused Projects

These two projects have come into being in slightly different ways and are very different in nature. The idea has been to identify somewhat more unusual groups of young people or to include certain desirable aspects in the study. These projects have been conducted for shorter periods of time.

---

1   In the chapters where this material is used, I have chosen to use some quotations from the original studies. In some cases I have used more than just a short sample from the original study. On these occasions I have asked the researchers in question for permission to collect excerpts from their studies.

1. *Political lesbianism* (Camilla Kolm, MSc in psychology). The aim of this project was to study how young women who choose to become lesbians based on their political convictions discuss this choice. How do they view sexuality, coming-out processes and the formation of gender? (n=9).
2. *Japanese youth culture, sexuality and identity* (Noriko Kurube, PhD in social work). This study was the result of an international collaboration and an invitation from a Japanese university. In connection with this collaboration, a pilot study was conducted using the above-mentioned Swedish survey, translated into Japanese (n=178). In addition, the research group conducted a number of group interviews with young Japanese people (n=30).

Kolm's study of political lesbians has a central position in our study and in the book. What is important here is the young women's discovery that it is possible to do gender, that is to construct a desirable identity, thereby questioning large parts of a more essentialistic understanding of gender. The Japanese study has been used primarily in the final chapter to allow a wider discussion of global sexuality.

Student Projects

During the course of the project, a number of undergraduate students have become interested in the questions posed in the overall framework of the project. This interest has resulted in a number of essays from different university programmes. The following is a summary of these essays:

1. *Religion, youth and sexuality* (Jessica Persson, BSc in Behavioural Science). This essay dealt with how young people involved in the Swedish Free Church discussed and gave shape to their sexuality (n=9).
2. *Identity, politics and sexuality in a small city* (Birgitta Larsson and Anna-Carin Lindh, BSc in Behavioural Science). The starting point of this essay was a group of six young feminist women living in a small Swedish city (n=6).
3. *Riot Grrls and feminism* (Sabina Ostermark, BSc in Cultural Studies). This essay dealt with material from the media, particularly different types of fanzines.
4. *Heterosexual love relations* (Lina Paulsson, MSc in Psychology). The purpose of this project was to study and deconstruct young men's views on heterosexual love (n=10).

All of the essay projects have been used to provide a picture of how young feminists do gender. They form the foundation of the study's ambition to examine and provide a contemporary picture of young feminine sexuality and identity.

Associated Projects

Finally, the project group was in contact with a number of doctoral students and researchers who published their own results within the framework of the project's published works. These contributions from associated projects have added extra dimensions to the atmosphere surrounding the project as well as complementary in-depth studies in areas not covered in our design.

1. *Young women, class and sexuality* (Fanny Ambjörnsson, PhD in Social Anthropology). Ambjörnsson contributed a chapter to the book *The Transformations of Sexuality* (*Sexualitetens omvandlingar*, 2003). This chapter focused on young women's ways of using and reconstructing sexually charged words. Here, Ambjörnsson analysed young women's resistance to sexism and repression. In her dissertation, Ambjörnsson used a strong class perspective (n=40).

2. *Ethnicity, race and sexuality* (Jesper Fundberg, PhD in Ethnology). Fundberg contributed a chapter to the book *The Transformations of Masculinity* (*Manlighetens omvandlingar*, Johansson 2005). This chapter focused on how young men with immigrant backgrounds use and negotiate by means of their sexuality. The study was conducted in a public market and comprised participant observations.

3. *Masculinity and feminism I* (Anna Hedenus, PhD student in Sociology). This is one of two contributions focused on how young men who express feminist views conceptualize gender, masculinity and sexuality. It is based on the author's Master's thesis in sociology (n=7).

4. *Masculinity and feminism II* (Cathrin Wasshede, PhD student in Sociology). In her dissertation, Wasshede investigates how men who are involved in politically radical leftist movements construct gender, sexuality and identity (n=25).

5. *Bisexual men* (Hanna Bertilsdotter, PhD student in Sociology). Bertilsdotter helped to prepare the project's grant application, but has primarily worked somewhat peripherally to the project. She is fully funded within the framework of gender studies. Bertilsdotter is working on a dissertation on young bisexual men (n=20).

6. *Media images of masculinity* (Anja Hirdman, PhD in Media Studies). Hirdman's study provides a contemporary picture of how young men are presented and portrayed in the media. She also discusses the aesthetization of the male body and the extent to which this is a question of a new masculinity.

Within the framework of the project, we have had the great advantage of working with a number of highly qualified researchers. All of them have contributed to the books published in connection with the project. In many respects, these researchers have helped us fill in the gaps and enabled us to broaden our picture of how young people create and do gender.

The Explorative Approach

This methods chapter is primarily intended to give the reader an understanding of the studies that form the foundation of the project as well as to give a picture of the context of the project. Another aim is to give a clearer picture of the research design. Our ambition has been to get an overall grasp on recent research on youth and sexuality conducted primarily in Sweden, but also in other nearby countries. In order to uphold this level of ambition, we have had to both work with more long-term projects and be prepared to absorb other research being carried out in our immediate vicinity.

As a whole, the project has not been based on well-delimited questions. Instead, the design has gradually evolved and the methods used are characterized by great variation. This does not imply, however, that the project has been lacking in direction, theoretical grounding or specific questions. We wish to see it as an explorative project, aimed at placing the results of different studies in a larger context. An additional ambition has been to capture some of the stability that characterizes today's youth culture, particularly with regard to how factors such as class, ethnicity and gender help to give shape to sexuality. Yet another parallel goal has been to be open to new things and to capture tendencies toward change. This dual ambition has also coloured the design of the project. One could say that the foundation of the project has been gradually widened to allow more comprehensive analyses of today's youth culture – with a particular focus on gender and sexuality, of course.

Another important ambition within the framework of the project has been to deconstruct and question many of the varyingly given contemporary conceptions of gender, youth and sexuality. This aspect per se has been a driving force; it has guided data collection and the contacts we have made with other scholars. This questioning of conceptions has been manifested in different ways, for example in the form of choice of study object or choice of interpretative frameworks. Most of the researchers and students connected to the project have based their work on a social constructivist perspective on gender. The project as a whole has been influenced primarily by post-structuralistic theory construction. At the same time, many of the authors and researchers have a strong background in more general sociological theories. Thus, deconstruction of 'the given' has occurred in relation to a broader and perhaps more classic sociological understanding of everyday life, gender and society. The theoretical perspective underlying the project is discussed in more detail in the book's conclusion section.

References

Abott, P. and Wallace, C. (1991), *Gender, Power and Sexuality* (London: Macmillan and Aldershot: Avebury).

Ambjörnsson, F. (2003), 'Kom nu hora, så går vi! Om svar på tal, utmanande beteenden och andra smakstrategier', in Johansson, T. and Lalander, P. (eds), *Sexualitetens omvandlingar. Politisk lesbiskhet, unga kristna och machokulturer* (Gothenburg: Daidalos).

Ambjörnsson, F. (2004), *I en klass för sig. Genus, klass och sexualitet bland gymnasietjejer* (Stockholm: Ordfront).

Andersson, Å. (2003), *Inte samma lika. Identifikation hos tonårsflickor i en multietnisk stadsdel* (Stockholm/Stehag: Symposion).

Andreasson, J. (2003), 'Brudar, bärs och bögar – maskulinitet och sexualitet i en enkönad miljö', in Johansson, T. and Lalander, P. (eds), *Sexualitetens omvandlingar. Politisk lesbiskhet, unga kristna oc h machokulturer* (Gothenburg: Daidalos).

Andreasson, J. (2005), 'Mellan svett och mascara. Maskulinitet i ett kvinnligt fotbollslag', in Johansson, T. (ed.), *Manlighetens omvandlingar. Ungdom, sexualitet och kön I heteronormativitetens gränstrakter* (Gothenburg: Daidalos).

Assiter, A. (1989), *Pornography, Feminism and the Individual* (London: Pluto).

Back, L. (1996), *New Ethnicities and Urban Culture. Racism and Multiculture in Young Lives* (London: UCL Press).

Bäckman, M. (2003), *Kön och känsla. Samlevnadsundervisning och ungdomars tankar om sexualitet* (Stockholm: Makadam förlag).

Bataille, G. (1957/1987), *Eroticism* (New York: Marion Boyars).

Baudrillard, J. (1977/1990), *Seduction* (London: Macmillan).

Baudrillard, J. (1983), *Simulations* (New York: Semiotext).

Baudrillard, J. (1990), *Amerika* (Gothenburg: Korpen).

Baudrillard, J. (1993a), *The Transparency of Evil. Essays on Extreme Phenomena* (New York: Semiotext).

Baudrillard, J. (1993b), *Symbolic Exchange and Death* (London: Sage).

Bauman, Z. (1990), *Modernity and Ambivalence* (Cambridge: Polity Press).

Bauman, Z. (1999), 'On Postmodern Uses of Sex', in Featherstone, M. (ed.), *Love and Eroticism* (London: Sage).

Bengtsson, M. (2001), *Tid, rum, kön och identitet* (Lund: Studentlitteratur).

Berg, L. (1999), *Lagom är bäst. Unga tjejers syn på sexualitet och pornografi* (Uppsala: Department of Sociology, Uppsala University).

Berger, P., Berger, B. and Kellner, H. (1974), *The Homeless Mind. Modernization and Consciousness* (New York: Vintage Books).

Bertilsdotter, H. (2003), 'Att fetischera det "normala" Bisexualitet utifrån några unga mäns berättelser', in Johansson, T. and Lalander, P. (eds), *Sexualitetens omvandlingar. Politisk lesbiskhet, unga kristna och machokulturer* (Gothenburg: Daidalos).

Bertilsdotter, H. (2005), 'En särskild sort öppen manlig (hetero)sexualitet', in Johansson, T. (ed.), *Manlighetens omvandlingar. Ungdom, sexualitet och kön i heteronormativitetens gränstrakter* (Gothenburg: Daidalos).

Butler, J. (1990), *Gender Trouble. Feminism and the Subversion of Identity* (London: Routledge).

Butler, R. (1999), *Jean Baudrillard* (London: Routledge).

Centervall, E. (2000), *'Kärlek känns! Förstår du'. Samtal om sexualitet och samlevnad i skolan* (Stockholm: Liber).

Connell, R.W. (1995), *Masculinities* (Cambridge: Polity Press).

Connell, R.W. (2000), *The Men and the Boys* (Cambridge: Polity Press).

Coupland, D. (1996), *Microserfs* (London: Flamingo).

Crosson, C. (1998), 'Den reaktionära kampen mot pornografin', *Arbetaren* 1.

de Beauvoir, S. (1949/1972), *The Second Sex* (Harmondsworth: Penguin Classics).

Dew, C.J. (1996), *Sexuality and Modern Western Culture* (New York: Twayne).

Douglas, M. (1966), *Purity and Danger. An Analysis of the Concepts of Pollution* (New York: Routledge).

Dworkin, A. (1991), 'Pornografi-Kriget mot kvinnor', in *Pornografi – verklighet eller fantasi?* (Stockholm: Riksorganisationen för Kvinnojourer i Sverige (ROKS)).

Dworkin, A. (1997), *Life and Death* (New York: Free Press).

Einarsson, J. and Hultman, T.G. (1984), *God morgon pojkar och flickor. Om språk och kön i skolan* (Lund: Gleerups).

Elias, N. (1939/1982), *The Civilising Process. State Formation and Civilisation* (Oxford: Blackwell).

Erikson, E.H. (1985), *The Life Cycle Completed. A Review* (New York: W.W. Norton).

Ewen, S. (1988), *All Consuming Images. The Politics of Style in Contemporary Culture* (New York: Basic Books).

Forsberg, M. (2000), *Ungdomar och sexualitet – en kunskapsöversikt år 2000* (Stockholm: Folkhälsoinstitutet, Report 15).

Forsberg, M. (2005), *Brunetter och Blondiner. Om ungdom och sexualitet i det mångkulturella Sverige* (Gothenburg: Institutionen för socialt arbete).

Foucault, M. (1976), *Sexualitetens historia I: Viljan att veta* (Stockholm: Gidlunds).

Foucault, M. (1978), *The History of Sexuality I: The Will to Knowledge* (Harmondsworth: Penguin Books).

Foucault, M. (1987a), *The History of Sexuality II: The Use of Pleasure* (Harmondsworth: Penguin Books).

Foucault, M. (1987b), *The History of Sexuality III: The Care of the Self* (Harmondsworth: Penguin Books).

Francis, B. (2000), *Boys, Girls and Achievement. Addressing the Classroom Issues* (London: Routledge).

Francis, B. and Skelton, C. (eds) (2001), *Investigating Gender. Contemporary Perspectives in Education* (Buckingham: Open University Press).

Freud, S. (1932/1989), *Civilization and its Discontents. The Standard Edition* (New York: W.W. Norton).

Frisell, A. (1996), *Kärlek utan sex går an ... men inte sex utan kärlek. Om gymnasieflickors tankar kring kärlek och sexualitet* (Stockholm: Mångkulturellt centrum).

Frosh, S., Phoenix, A. and Pattman, R. (2002), *Young Masculinities. Understanding Boys in Contemporary Society* (London: Palgrave).

Frykman, J. and Löfgren, O. (1979), *Den kultiverade människan* (Lund: Glerups förlag).

Ganetz, H. (1992), 'Butiken, hemmet och kvinnligheten som maskerad. Drivkrafter och platser för kvinnligt stilskapande', in Fornäs, J., Boethius, U., Ganetz, H. and Reimer, B. (eds), *Unga stilar och uttrycksformer* (Stockholm/Stehag: Symposion).

Garber, M. (2000), *Bisexuality and the Eroticism of Everyday Life* (New York: Routledge).

Giddens, A. (1991), *Modernity and Self-Identity. Self and Society in Late Modern Societies* (Cambridge: Polity Press).

Giddens, A. (1992), *The Transformation of Intimacy* (Cambridge: Polity Press).

Gilbert, R. and Gilbert, P. (1998), *Masculinities Goes to School* (New York: Routledge).

Green, K. and Taormino, T. (eds) (1997), *A Girl's Guide to Taking Over the World* (New York: St Martin's Griffin).

Griffin, C. (1985), *Typical Girls?: Young Women from the School to the Job Market* (London: Routledge & Kegan Paul).

Häggström-Nordin, E. (2005), *World's Apart? Sexual Behaviour, Contraceptive Use, and Pornography Consumption among Young Women and Men* (Uppsala Universitet: Akademisk avhandling).

Håkansson, G. (1999), 'Om pornografi', *Res Publica* 1.

Hall, S. (1999), 'Kodning och avkodning', in Johansson, T., Sernhede, O. and Trondman, M. (eds), *Samtidskultur. Karaoke, karnevaler och kulturella koder* (Nora: Nya Doxa).

Hammarén, N. (2003), 'Horor, players och de Andra. Killar och sexualitet i det nya Sverige', in Johansson, T. and Lalander, P. (eds), *Sexualitetens omvandlingar. Politisk lesbiskhet, unga kristna och machokulturer* (Gothenburg: Daidalos).

Hammarén, N. (2005), 'Välkommen till förorten om du vågar! Territorialitet och manlighet', in Johansson, T. (ed.), *Manlighetens omvandlingar. Ungdo, sexualitet och kön I heteronormativitetens gränstrakter* (Gothenburg: Daidalos).

Hammarén, N. and Johansson, T. (2001), *Ungdom och sexualitet i gränslandet. Delrapport I. Ung och kåt? Om ungdomars sexuella berättelser* (Skövde: Polytechnic of Skövde, report 1).

140   The Transformation of Sexuality

Hammarén, N. and Johansson, T. (2002), *Könsordning eller könsoordning? Ungdomens sexuella landskap* (Gothenburg: Centre of Cultural Studies, research report 2).

Hammarén, N. and Johansson, T. (2005), 'Gender order or disorder?', in Månson, S.-A. and Clothilde, C. *Social Work in Cuba and Sweden. Achievements and Prospects* (Gothenburg: Department of Social Work University of Gothenburg).

Haraway, D. (1990), 'A Cyborg Manifesto. Science, Technology and Socialist Feminism in the 1980s', in Nicholson, L.J. (ed.), *Feminism/Postmodernism* (London: Routledge).

Harris, A. (ed.) (2004), *All About the Girl. Culture, Power and Identity* (New York: Routledge).

Hawkes, G. (1996), *A Sociology of Sex and Sexuality* (Milton Keynes: Open University Press).

Hebdige, D. (1979), *Subculture. The Meaning of Style* (London: Routledge).

Hedenus, A. (2005), 'Med eller emot? De manliga feministernas dilemma', in Johansson, T. (ed.), *Manlighetens omvandlingar. Ungdom, sexualitet och kön I heteronormativitetens gränstrakter* (Gothenburg: Daidalos).

Helmius, G. (1990), *Mogen för sex? Det sexuella restriktiviserande samhället och ungdomars heterosexuella glädje* (Uppsala: Department of Sociology, Uppsala University).

Henriksson, B. and Lundahl, P. (1993), *Ungdom, sexualitet och könsroller* (Gothenburg: Department of Social Work, Gothenburg University, report 1993:6).

Herlitz, C. (2001), *Allmänheten och hiv/aids – kunskaper, attityder och beteenden 1989 – 2000* (Stockholm: Folkhälsoinstitutet).

Hite, S. (1981), *The Hite Report on Male Sexuality* (New York: Balantine).

Holland, J., Ramazanoglu, C., Sharpe, S. and Thomson, R. (1998), *The Male in the Head. Young People, Heterosexuality and Power* (London: Tufnell Press).

hooks, b. (1992), 'Att äta den andre. Begär och motstånd', in Johansson, T., Sernhede, O. and Trondman, M. (eds), *Samtidskultur. Karaoke, karnevaler och kulturella koder* (Lund: Nya Doxa).

Hornby, N. (1995), *High Fidelity* (Stockholm: Månpocket).

Jeffner, S. (1997), *'Liksom våldtäkt typ' om betydelsen av kön och heterosexualitet för ungdomars förståelse av våldtäkt* (Uppsala: Department of Sociology, Uppsala University).

Johansson, L. (2000), 'Vi fick veta saker om sex', in Skugge, L.N., Olsson, B. and Zilg, B. (eds), *Fittstim* (Stockholm: DN bokförlag).

Johansson, T. (1998), *Den skulpterade kroppen. Gymkultur, friskvård och estetik* (Stockholm: Carlssons förlag).

Johansson, T. (2000), *Det första könet? Mansforskning som reflexiv praktik* (Lund: Studentlitteratur).

Johansson, T. (2002), *Bilder av självet* (Stockholm: Natur och Kultur).

Johansson, T. (ed.) (2005), *Manlighetens omvandlingar – ungdom, sexualitet och kön i heteronormativitetens gränstrakter* (Gothenburg: Daidalos).

Johansson, T. and Hammarén, N. (forthcoming), 'Hegemonic Masculinity and Pornography. Young People's Attitudes and Relations Towards Pornography', *Journal of Men's Studies*.

Johansson, T. and Lalander, P. (eds) (2003), *Sexualitetens omvandlingar. Politisk lesbiskhet, unga kristna och machokulturer* (Gothenburg: Daidalos).

Johansson, T. and Miegel, F. (1992), *Do the Right Thing. Lifestyle and Identity in Contemporary Swedish Youth Culture* (Stockholm: Almqvist and Wiksell International).

Kolm, C. (2003), 'Politisk lesbisk i senmodern tid', in Johansson, T. and Lalander, P. (eds), *Sexualitetens omvandlingar. Politisk lesbiskhet, unga kristna och machokulturer* (Gothenburg: Daidalos).

Kroger, J. (1989), *Identity in Adolescence. The Balance between Self and Other* (New York: Routledge).

Kroker, A. and Kroker, M. (1988), *Body Invaders. Sexuality and the Postmodern Condition* (London: Macmillan).

Kvarning, M. (1998) 'Vi är de nya porrfeministerna', *Aftonbladet* 26 August.

Larsson, B. and Lindh, A.-C. (2003), '"Det har hänt att man har blivit kallad feministhora". Identitet, sexulitet och politik I småstad', in Johansson, T. and Lalander, P. (eds), *Sexualitetens omvandlingar. Politisk lesbiskhet, unga kristna oc h machokulturer* (Gothenburg: Daidalos).

Lees, S. (1993), *Sugar and Spice. Sexuality and Adolescent Girls* (Harmondsworth: Penguin Books).

Leonard, M. (1998), 'Paper Planes. Travelling the New Grrrl Geographies', in Skelton, T. and Valentine, G. (eds), *Cool places. Geographies of Youth Cultures* (London: Routledge).

Lewin, B. (1991), *Att omplantera sexualiteten. Om latinamerikanska ungdomars sexuella socialisation i Sverige* (Uppsala: Department of Sociology, Uppsala University).

Lewin, B. and Helmius, G. (1983), *Ungdom och sexualitet. En sociologisk studie avd ungdomars sexuella föreställningar och erfarenheter* (Uppsala: Department of Sociology, Uppsala University).

Lindqvist, S. (1981), *En älskares dagbok* (Stockholm: Bonniers).

Lundahl, P. (1998), *Lesbisk identitet* (Stockholm: Carlssons förlag).

Lundgren, E., Heimer, G., Westerstrand, J. and Kalliokoski, A.-M. (2001), *Slagen dam. Mäns våld mot kvinnor – en omfångsundersökning* (Stockholm: Fritzes).

Mac an Ghaill, M. (1997), *The Making of Men. Masculinities, Sexualities and Schooling* (Buckingham: Open University Press).

Månsson, S.-A., Danebeck, K., Tikkanen, R. and Löfgren-Mårtensson, L. (2003), *Kärlek och sex på Internet* (Gothenburg: Gothenburg University, Nätsexprojektet 2003:1).

Martin, K. (1996), *Puberty, Sexuality, and the Self. Girls and Boys at Adolescence* (London: Routledge).

McLaren, A. (1999), *Twentieth Century Sexuality. A History* (Oxford: Blackwell).

McLuhan, M. (1964), *Understanding Media. The Extensions of Man* (New York: Penguin Books).

McNair, B. (2002), *Striptease Culture. Sex, Media and the Democratisation of Desire* (New York: Routledge).

McRobbie, A. (1989), 'En feministisk kritik av subkultur-forskningen', in Fornäs, J., Lindberg, U. and Sernhede, O. (eds), *Ungdomskultur: Identitet och motstånd* (Stockholm/Stehag: Symposion).

McRobbie, A. and Garber, J. (1986), 'Piger og subkulturer', in Bay, J. and Drotner, K. (eds), *Ungdom, en stil, et liv* (Copenhagen: Tiderne skrifter).

Mestrović, S.G. (1997), *Postemotional Society* (London: Sage).

Meyrowitz, J. (1985), *No Sense of Place. The Impact of Electronic Media on Social Behavior* (Oxford: Oxford University Press).

Morris-Roberts, K. (2004), 'Colluding in "Compulsory Heterosexuality"? Doing Research with Young Women at School', in Harris, A. (ed.), *All About the Girl. Culture, Power and Identity* (New York: Routledge).

Nagel, J. (2003), *Race, Ethnicity and Sexuality. Intimate Intersections, Forbidden Frontiers* (New York: Oxford University Press).

Nixon, S. (1996), *Hard Looks. Masculinity, Spectatorship and Contemporary Consumption* (London: UCL Press).

Nordenmark, L. (2000), 'Livsskedesbeskrivningar', in Sundström, K. (ed.), *Hur gör dom andra? Om sexualitet och samlevnad på 1990 – talet* (Stockholm: Folkhälsoinstitutet, report 7).

O'Donnell, M. and Sharpe, S. (2000), *Uncertain Masculinities. Youth, Ethnicity and Class in Contemporary Britain* (London: Routledge).

Olvivaria, J. (2003), *Varones Adolescentes: Género, Identidades y sexualidades en América Latina* (Santiago de Chile: UNFPA. FLASCO).

Ostermark, S. (2003), 'Rött läppstift är också politik. Fanzines och feminism', in Johansson, T. and Lalander, P. (eds.), *Sexualitetens omvandlingar. Politisk lesbiskhet, unga kristna och machokulturer* (Gothenburg: Daidalos).

Öhrn, E. (1991), *Könsmönster i klassrumsinteraktion. En observations- och intervjustudie av högstadieelevers lärarkontakter* (Gothenburg: Acta Universittatis Gothemburgensis).

Öhrn, E. (1998), 'Gender and Power in School: On Girls' Open Resistance', *Social Psychology of Education* 1.

Öhrn, E. (2000), 'Changing Patterns? Reflections on Contemporary Swedish Research and Debate on Gender and Education', *Nora* 3.

Paecter, C. (2000), *Changing School Subjects. Power, Gender and Curriculum* (Buckingham: Open University Press).

Paulsson, L. (2005), '"Hon såg mig som en man liksom". Unga mäns identitetsskapande I heterosexuella relationer', in Johansson, T. (ed.), *Manlighetens omvandlingar. Ungdom, sexualitet och kön I heteronormativitetens gränstrakter* (Gothenburg: Daidalos).

Plummer, K. (1995), *Telling Sexual Stories. Power, Change and Social Worlds* (London: Routledge).

Plummer, K. (1996), 'Intimate Citizenship and the Culture of Sexual Story Telling', in Weeks, J. and Holland, J. (1996) *Sexual Cultures. Communities, Values and Intimacy* (London: Macmillan).

Rogala, C. and Tydén, T. (1999), *Unga kvinnors sexualvanor* (Stockholm: Folkhälsoinstitutet).

Rogala, C. and Tydén, T. (2001), *Unga mäns sexualvanor* (Stockholm: Folkhälsoinstitutet).

Ronningstam, E. (1988), *Studies on Narcisstisic Disturbances* (Stockholm: Natur och Kultur).

Said, E. (1978/1993), *Orientalism* (Stockholm: Bonniers).

Sernhede, O. (1998), 'I väntan på Mandela – om invandrarkillars utanförskap och motståndskulturer', *Krut* 2.

Sernhede, O. (2002), *Alienation is my Nation. Hiphop och unga mäns utanförskap I det nya Sverige* (Stockholm: Ordfront förlag).

Simmel, G. (1900/1990), *The Philosophy of Money* (London: Routledge).

Skugge, L.N., Olsson, B. and Zilg, B. (eds) (1999), *Fittstim* (Stockholm: DN bokförlag).

Sörensen, N.U. (2000), *Pikstormene* (Roskilde: Roskilde University).

Steinberg, D.L., Epstein, D. and Johnsson, R. (1997), *Border Patrols. Policing the Boundaries of Heterosexuality* (London: Casell).

Strossen, N. (1995), *Defending Pornography. Free Speech, Sex, and the Fight for Women's Rights* (New York: Scribner).

Svenberg, J. (2000), 'Tack Gud att jag är lesbisk', in Skugge, L.N., Olsson, B. and Zilg, B. (eds) *Fittstim* (Stockholm: DN bokförlag).

Svensson, K. (1993), 'Våld, dominans och sexualitet', in *Tre rapporter om pornografi* (Stockholm: RFSU).

Swain, J. (2005), 'Masculinities in Education', in Kimmel, M.S., Hearn, J. and Connell, R.W. (eds), *Handbook of Men and Masculinities* (London: Sage).

Taylor, T.D. (1997), *Global Pop, World Music, World Markets* (London: Routledge).

Turkle, S. (1996), *Life on the Screen. Identity in the Age of the Internet* (London: Weidenfeld & Nicolson).

Virilio, P. (1991), *The Lost Dimension* (New York: Semiotext).

Virilio, P. (2000), *Polar Inertia* (London: Sage).

Wasshede, C. (2005), 'Skägg eller kjol? Unga aktivistmän om maskulinitet och femininitet', in Johansson, T. (ed.), *Manlighetens omvandlingar. Ungdom, sexualitet och kön I heteronormativitetens gränstrakter* (Gothenburg: Daidalos).

Weeks, J. (1985), *Sexuality and its Discontents. Meanings, Myths & Modern Sexuality* (London: Routledge & Kegan Paul).

Weeks, J. (1987), 'Questions of Identity', in Caplan, P. (ed.), *The Cultural Construction of Sexuality* (London: Tavistock Publications).

Weeks, J. (2000), *Making Sexual History* (Cambridge: Polity Press).

Williams, L. (1989), *Hard Core. Power, Pleasure and the Frenzy of the Visible* (Berkeley: University of California Press).

Williams, L. (1999), 'Fetischism och hardcore. Marx, Freud och "kassascenen"', *Res Publica* 1/99. First printed in Williams, L. (1989), *Hard Core. Power, Pleasure and the Frenzy of the Visible* (Berkeley: University of California Press).

Willis, P. (1977), *Learning to Labour. How Working Class Kids Get Working Class Jobs* (Cambridge: Polity Press).

Wolpe, A.M. (1988), *Within School Walls. The Role of Discipline, Sexuality and the Curriculum* (London: Routledge).

Wulff, H. (1988), *Twenty Girls. Growing up, Ethnicity, and Excitement in a South London Microculture* (Stockholm: York Press, Stockholm Studies in Social Anthropology).

Ziehe, T. (1989), *Kulturanalyser – Ungdom, utbildning och modernitet* (Stockholm/ Stehag: Symposium).

Index

DATE DUE

DEMCO, INC. 38-2931